Praise for
Listen, Listen, Speak

"Jay Kim does it again in *Listen, Listen, Speak*. He equips us to navigate communication and media pressures which are unrelenting and increasing…Jay brings a tone, clarity, and humor that is water to a thirsty soul. I highly recommend *Listen, Listen, Speak*."

—Steve Cuss, founder of *Capable Life* and author of *Managing Leadership Anxiety*

"Somewhere amid all the noise of opinions and divisions, we stopped listening. And we stopped speaking for fear that we too would simply add to the fray. But Jay Kim, as he so often does, offers us a better way…This is a book for our moment."

—Glenn Packiam, lead pastor at Rock Harbor and author of *The Resilient Pastor*

"*Listen, Listen, Speak* is a fresh word. This book is not the same old message about avoiding social media and the news, or escaping from the 'placeless places' that are discipling us. Rather, author and pastor Jay Kim beckons the reader to stay rooted in holy listening, in the actual places we are planted, and in God's very real presence—so that when we finally speak, we do so as the 'Good News' people God has declared us to be. Imagine quieting the noise of your world long enough to truly listen to it. This is the beautiful paradox Jay Kim invites the willing reader into."

—Aubrey Sampson, pastor and author of
The Louder Song and *Known*

"We live in a speak-first, listen-later world. Jay's book title alone is challenging but the content is transforming. If you've been looking for a way to hear from God amid all the chaos, this book is for you."

—Ashley Wooldridge, senior pastor of
Christ's Church of the Valley

"In a world that is constantly talking (more accurately, shouting), how do we listen? Not just to others, but to the voice of God? I love what my brother Jay shares with us in *Listen, Listen, Speak*. Jay gives us wisdom and practical advice on how to navigate the chaos we have to sift through every day. I honestly feel like this book was written for me. Do yourself a favor and grab a copy today!"

—Adam Weber, lead pastor of Embrace Church,
author, and podcast host

"With compassion and conviction, Jay Kim cuts through the noise of our day and gives us hope, vulnerability, and a path forward. I found myself pausing and praying to attune my ears and heart to God because of Jay's refreshing perspective."

—Amy Seiffert, Bible teacher and author of *Starved* and *Grace Looks Amazing on You*

"Jay Kim writes a wonderfully personal reflection done with deep biblical and cultural insight helping us understand the role of listening to the gentle whispers of the Lord God in the cacophony of our world before moving to speaking the good news of Jesus with a voice constantly curated by Word and Spirit in the community of the king."

—Gerry Breshears, professor of theology at Western Seminary

"Jay has written a book that is a must-read in our current cultural mood. Followers of Jesus must lead the way in breaking from our digital addictions and becoming communities that know how to listen with love and speak with truth. I'm thankful for this book and highly recommend it."

—Dave Lomas, pastor at Reality SF and author of *The Truest Thing About You*

"In this wonderful book, Jay Kim offers spiritual simplicity as the antidote to life's growing complexities. Prayer, the Bible, and spiritual community are not merely add-ons to our life with God; rather, they are what this life is built on. In an age of distraction and division, learning to listen to God and others can be your superpower and perhaps the only way you will ever have something to say."

—Jarrett Stevens, co-founding pastor of Soul City Church
and author of *Praying Through* and *Four Small Words*

"*Listen, Listen, Speak* invites us all to follow Jesus from the quiet place and then courageously live from the overflow of that place with prayerful intention to usher in the hope-filled beauty of the Kingdom of Heaven in the here and now."

—Brian Wurzell, pastor of creative programming
at Passion City Church

Listen, Listen, Speak

Listen, Listen, Speak

*Hearing God and Being Heard
in a Noisy World*

Jay Y. Kim

FaithWords

New York   Nashville

FaithWords
Hachette Book Group
1290 Avenue of the Americas, New York, NY 10104
faithwords.com
twitter.com/faithwords

First Edition: April 2024

FaithWords is a division of Hachette Book Group, Inc.
The FaithWords name and logo are registered trademarks of Hachette Book Group, Inc.

The publisher is not responsible for websites (or their content) that are not owned by the publisher.

The Hachette Speakers Bureau provides a wide range of authors for speaking events. To find out more, go to hachettespeakersbureau.com or email HachetteSpeakers@hbgusa.com.

FaithWords books may be purchased in bulk for business, educational, or promotional use. For information, please contact your local bookseller or the Hachette Book Group Special Markets Department at special.markets@hbgusa.com.

Library of Congress Cataloging-in-Publication Data
Names: Kim, Jay Y., 1979- author.
Title: Listen, listen, speak : hearing god and being heard in a noisy world / Jay Y. Kim.
Description: First edition. | New York : FaithWords, 2024. |
Includes bibliographical references.
Identifiers: LCCN 2023041039 | ISBN 9781546004998 (hardcover) |
ISBN 9781546005018 (ebook)
Subjects: LCSH: Bible. New Testament. | Jesus Christ. | Christian life. | Social media. |
Misinformation.
Classification: LCC BS2001 .K46 2024 | DDC 225—dc23/eng/20231127
LC record available at https://lccn.loc.gov/2023041039

ISBNs: 9781546004998 (hardcover), 9781546005018 (ebook)

Printed in the United States of America

LSC-C

Printing 1, 2024

For Simon, my sweet boy.
May you listen well and hear the voice
of your Father in heaven,
whose grace you cannot comprehend,
whose love you cannot outrun.

Contents

Listen, Listen, Speak

Cacophony and Chaos

If you and I were speaking face-to-face, assuming we were talking at an average volume, our conversation would register at about 60 decibels. A quiet library is 40 decibels, and a whisper, about 30 decibels. At the other end of the spectrum, a crying baby is 110 decibels, and an airplane at takeoff is 140 decibels. I'm not sure of the decibel level of a crying baby on an airplane, but grace and peace to you, young parents. I've been there.

The quietest sound a person with average hearing can hear is zero decibels. But there are rooms called anechoic (meaning "no echo") chambers where silence conquers sound. The quietest place on earth is the anechoic chamber at the Microsoft office in Redmond, Washington. Its decibel reading: −20 decibels. That's *negative* twenty decibels. After just a few moments inside, you begin to hear your own heart beating. A few minutes more and you can hear the blood flowing through your body and the grinding of your bones with even the slightest movement. Just a short while in the chamber causes significant disorientation as your eyes see a room but your ears tell your brain that you're nowhere at all. Hundraj Gopal, the principal designer of the chamber, notes that "Most people find the absence of sound deafening."[1]

The deafening absence of sound. What a thought.

We live in a noisy world. This is literally true, as urbanization moves more and more people into congested cities and suburbs and away from the quieter sprawls of rural lands. But it's even more true in our digital world of media. In the past decade, media consumption has increased by more than 20 percent. The most dramatic shift has come by way of the smartphone. In 2011, the average person spent forty-five minutes a day on their phone. Today, that number is well over four hours, an increase of more than 500 percent.[2] For the nearly four billion social media users around the world, much if not most of this time is spent jostling around in the cacophony and chaos of our feeds.

From political pundits, media personalities, and online influencers to armchair social commentators and recreational conspiracy theorists, everyone has something to say, all the time, about everything. This includes you and me. As the comedian Bo Burnham asks, "Is it necessary that every single person on this planet expresses every single opinion that they have on every single thing that occurs all at the same time? Is that, is *that*, necessary?"[3] We laugh. But sadly, the answer seems to be a resounding yes, which is no laughing matter. Our feeds, coupled with the relentless pings of text messages and emails, leave us so accustomed to sound that any hint of quiet or stillness becomes radically disorienting. This is just as true for the Baby Boomer living in a rural Midwestern town as it is for the young digital native living in Silicon Valley. We are all citizens of the age of noise.

So much talking. So little actually being heard.

So much chatter. So little actually being said.

And though there is a disturbing sort of comfort in the noise, we mostly find ourselves exhausted by it. Intuitively, we understand that human beings are not actually made to live this way. We long for sustained quiet to consider the most important things of life and, in turn, give us an effective and meaningful voice in a world of chatter. So the question is, how can we hear well and speak effectively in such an age of noise? For Christians, how are we to hear God through the cacophony and speak good news into the chaos?

A GENTLE WHISPER AND HOLDING ATTENTION

In 1 Kings 19, we read the story of a prophet named Elijah. The story is well known for its oft-quoted verse 12, which tells us that God speaks to Elijah in a "gentle whisper." More on that in a moment, but first, the backstory. Elijah was a prophet called to speak the truth of God to a culture immersed in idols. In the previous chapter, he confronted the false prophets of Baal, the primary idol of the day. Full of courage and conviction, Elijah stood atop a mountain, one man surrounded by hundreds, and prayed that God would prove himself in the sight of his enemies. In a definitive display of his authority and power, God sent down fire from the heavens, and Elijah slaughtered the false prophets. But then, the pagan queen of the land, Jezebel, in furious response, threatened to hunt down and kill Elijah. "Elijah was afraid and ran for his life" (1 Kings 19:3).

Elijah flees in fear and eventually finds himself on Mount Horeb. This is the same mountain where Moses had encountered God on several occasions during the Exodus story, sometimes called Mount Sinai. On this elevated plain where the divine meets the ordinary, God speaks into Elijah's fear and exhaustion.

> The Lord said, "Go out and stand on the mountain in the presence of the Lord, for the Lord is about to pass by." Then a great and powerful wind tore the mountains apart and shattered the rocks before the Lord, but the Lord was not in the wind. After the wind there was an earthquake, but the Lord was not in the earthquake. After the earthquake came a fire, but the Lord was not in the fire. And after the fire came a *gentle whisper.* (1 Kings 19:11–12, emphasis added)

Why a "gentle whisper"? God had just sent fire from heaven. This is the same God who'd parted seas and conquered enemies.

Straining to hear the voice of God speak to us in an age of

noise, we often find ourselves asking similar questions. Why doesn't God speak—big and bold? Why doesn't he shout above the noise in a way that's undeniable? Why does it seem so often that he's whispering, if speaking at all?

Many years ago, I found myself substitute teaching a group of second graders. Within minutes, I'd lost control of the room. These tiny little barely humans were running circles around me, screaming and yelling. A veteran teacher happened to walk by, and seeing my despair, she stepped in, calm, cool, and collected. Without saying a word, she stood tall in the middle of the classroom, raised a single hand in the air, and looked intently at the children. One by one the kids settled down and began sitting at her feet. Silence overwhelmed sound. This teacher held their attention not by joining the noisy fray but by transcending it with a calm and quiet presence.

Sometimes calm and quiet is exactly what's needed to cut through the noise. The twentieth-century theologian H. D. M. Spence describes God's gentle whisper this way: "Not in fire and sword and slaughter, but by a secret voice speaking to the conscience, will God regain His sway over the hearts of Israel."[4] I've come to believe that one of the fundamental reasons why we struggle to hear God speak is because we assume that his voice does and will always be loud and thunderous. We expect God to speak "in fire and sword and slaughter." We expect *volume*.

But there is a difference between *volume* and *clarity*. Just because something is loud does not mean it's clear. And though loudness often grabs our attention, it's clarity that holds our attention. Grabbing attention is transactional. Holding attention is relational. Our social media feeds grab our attention because of their offer of momentary escape. But God longs to speak to us clearly, not loudly, because he longs to hold our attention, not simply grab it; he desires relationship with us, not transaction.

Human attention works in a variety of ways. Imagine yourself walking into a room you believe to be empty. Without notice you hear a sudden "Hello!" You're startled. This form of attention is merely a reaction; it's a primal response. When we're startled, a small handful of neurons travels from the ears up the spine and to the brain in mere tenths of a second and initiates a defensive posture. This same neurological reaction and physiological response has been seen in every observed vertebrate. It's a baseline, animalistic sort of attention embedded in our DNA as a protective mechanism against threats. But this sort of attention is lost as quickly as it is gained. In other words, the startling auditory cue that grabs our attention rarely sustains and holds it.

But there's a more complex form of human attention that neuroscientists call top-down attention. Imagine hearing your name from across a noisy room. The auditory cue may have been faint, but it was also distinct. And it was your name. It involves you and therefore elicits an effortful search to find its source. When this happens, neurons travel down the pathway of your brain designed for complex work as you tune out other noises and lean into the distant sound drawing you in. Though the sound may have been a gentle whisper, so to speak, it captivates you and you push your way through the cacophony—the powerful wind, the earthquake, the fire—to find it. The whisper holds our attention.

Author and neuroscientist Seth Horowitz writes, "The richness of life doesn't lie in the loudness and the beat, but in the timbres and the variations that you can discern if you simply pay attention."[5] What is paying attention if not quieting competing sounds, leaning in, and listening close? This is exactly what God is after. Our inability to hear God isn't due to God's silence—he's speaking. It's due to the fact that we are not quieting competing sounds, leaning in, and listening close.

So how do we do this? What does this look and sound like in an age of noise?

THE TIMELESS WHISPER HAS BEEN HERE ALL ALONG

I grew up in the church but began genuinely following Jesus in college. After a season of deconstructing faith, I began a slow journey back toward God through a small group of guys I met with every Monday night. During that season of life,

I remember hearing God more clearly than at any other time. But his voice was never audible. I never awoke in the middle of the night, like Samuel, hearing my name called from the darkness. There was never a burning bush in the distance, beckoning me to draw near and listen close. His voice was simpler, more accessible, some would even say, more basic. During that season, I began learning to hear God by living a listening life.

That phrase, *a listening life*, sounds serene and effortless. In reality, it's anything but. Hearing God requires willful effort, not because God wants to make it hard on us but because God desires our attention, and attention demands that we relinquish all other pursuits. So we listen as an act of will, focusing our minds and hearts. We do this in a variety of ways, but three essential practices are paramount.

As the online personalities rage, *prayer* orients us toward the timeless voice of God.

As the pundits make their predictions, *Scripture* offers us the daily voice of God.

As the influencers cry, "See me," the *church* reminds us that God sees us.

While you might be thinking that prayer, Scripture, and church community are too simple to resolve the challenges we face, hang with me for a moment. I'm not suggesting that reading a few verses, reciting a handful of formulaic prayers, and going to church a couple times a month is the answer.

A disengaged, rote, going-through-the-motions approach to these three practices rarely leads to a life attuned to the voice of God. Consistency and repetition matter, of course. More than that, they're necessary. We practice, not just think or feel, our way toward hearing God. But in order for prayer, Scripture, and the church to be a means to hearing God, we first need to rethink and reimagine each, particularly in an age of noise.

In the following pages, we'll explore the challenges we face and how each of these ancient and timeless gifts—prayer, Scripture, church—can lead us to a listening life. But for now, there's a second issue at hand. Hearing is not enough. God does not speak for us to be inactive or idle. God speaks in order to send us back into the world with something to say.

GO BACK

After God speaks to Elijah in the gentle whisper, he instructs him this way: "Go back the way you came" (1 Kings 19:15). God sends Elijah back into the cacophony and chaos. He calls him back into the fray. God speaks to us in order that we might speak. As the prophet Jeremiah wrote, "The Lord reached out his hand and touched my mouth and said to me, 'I have put my words in your mouth'" (Jeremiah 1:9).

So what does it take to speak and to be heard in an age of noise? There are a variety of challenges we face, but two

in particular—social media and politics—are perplexing and
unnerving, especially as they intersect.

With respect to the first, Chamath Palihapitiya, former
vice president of user growth at Facebook, recently said, "We
are in a really bad state of affairs right now . . . [Social media]
is eroding the core foundation of how people behave by and
between each other."[6] Similarly, the writer Jaron Lanier says
that within social media, "[we] lose sight of the reality of what
[we're] doing because the immediate power struggle looms
larger than reality itself."[7]

Criticizing social media may feel like old hat at this point,
and that's fair. Its dangers have been discussed ad nauseam.
The problem is that most of us are still addicted. And when it
comes to speaking good news, our addiction is shackling us.
The word *addiction* comes from a Latin word that at the time
of Jesus was used to describe a person who'd been enslaved by
court ruling. In other words, it was the legal term for a slave.
Addicts are slaves. And slaves have no voice. Our addiction
to scrolling and swiping is stifling our ability to speak and
be heard. This is frighteningly true when it comes to politics.

The past several years have been the most challenging I've
faced in two decades as a pastor. There are several reasons,
but political division has been one of the primary culprits.
It's not that we shouldn't be political. It's that being political has taken on a whole new meaning in the digital age.
Matt Taibbi writes that when it comes to politics, both news
and social media "need you anxious, pre-pissed, addicted to

conflict. Moreover we need you to bring a series of assumptions every time you open a paper or turn on your phone, TV, or car radio. Without them, most of what we produce will seem illogical and offensive."[8] The mixture of our outrage, cynicism, and tribalism is the fuel that runs the 24/7 news and social media cycles. We energize it and then are in turn exhausted by it.

In large part because our technologies allow us to take out our angst on anyone, anywhere, anytime, an inversion has taken place. We often neglect our local communities, where we have the greatest opportunity to truly be heard, and instead, we yell into the vast expanse of the digital world, pontificating on the national and global issues of the day, all from the safe distance of our screens and devices—though rarely changing anyone's mind. Social media in particular beckons us to comment on things that aren't local to an audience that isn't local, and our voice fades and eventually succumbs to the cacophony. All the while, God calls us to "Seek the peace and prosperity of the city to which I have carried you" (Jeremiah 29:7).

In the latter chapters of this book, we'll explore these challenges of our culture in greater detail and consider how followers of Jesus can speak into the chaos. To a world on edge, defensive, and hurting, Christians have a responsibility to not only listen to God but also to speak good news in a way that can actually be heard.

Years ago, my friend Dave was studying in a journalism program in New York City. Dave is a big guy, about six foot four with an offensive lineman's build. One day on the subway, a man he describes as significantly bigger than he is bumbled onto the train, reeking of alcohol, with a brown paper bag in hand. The man began screaming obscenities to no one in particular. His anger steadily built. His belligerence began to edge toward violence. Dave remembers thinking, *I don't think I can take this guy if things get out of control.* The other passengers, paralyzed by fear, sat quiet and still, hoping to ignore the threat away. Then, a slight elderly man stood up and walked slowly toward the drunk and began to speak in a voice marked by convicted calm and gentle confidence.

"Are you drinking because you're sad?" the elder asked.

"What did you say to me!?!" replied the drunk.

"Are you drinking because you're sad? Because I remember when my wife died, I was so very sad, and I drank a lot. Are you sad?" the elder asked.

The drunk looked at the elder. As their eyes met, rage gave way to grace. Fury gave way to peace. An elderly man stood tall inside of a crowded New York City subway train and offered a new way forward for a fellow man in pain. He spoke good news into brokenness.

In spite of all the noise, God longs to speak and *is* speaking. But he is speaking so that we might speak in return. He is putting words in our mouths so that we might utter good news into the cacophony and chaos of a world on edge. This is the shared enterprise, the participatory work, the kingdom mission he's inviting all of us into.

In Jesus' own words, "Whoever has ears, let them hear" (Matthew 11:15).

May we open our ears to hear God in an age of noise.

May we open our mouths to speak good news into the cacophony and chaos.

PART I

Listen

One

God's Timeless Voice amid the Rage of Personalities

"You're doing the devil's work."

That was the subject line of the email. A congregant in our church, soon to leave our church, was furious. In the opening paragraphs he offered diatribe about my failures as a pastor and a leader. He wasn't totally wrong. Failure, at times, is a regular part of leading. But his critique felt personal, and I'd be lying if I said it wasn't hurtful. It was.

But this isn't about self-pity. By God's grace, I've grown more comfortable in my own skin in recent years. I've learned to find confidence in the fact that what God asks of me is faithfulness, not flawlessness, and an important part of faithfulness is leaning into the tension, not away from it, and pastoring into the mess, not around it. Serving and shepherding a local church congregation is a strange and beautiful gift. What made this instance so confusing and alarming was the reason for the anger.

This particular email had to do with our church's decision to adhere to our county's gathering regulations during the COVID-19 pandemic. Our elders and leadership team prayerfully considered all options, and in the end, we arrived at the conclusion that maintaining our relationship with county officials, built over many years of serving and engaging for the good of our city, was worth the inconvenience and loss of not gathering in person for a while.

Lots of people left our church, many of them voicing their displeasure on the way out. We grieved but felt a strong conviction that this was the path God was calling us to take. It wasn't a matter of doctrine or theology. Other churches in our city took a different approach. Some took the county to court and sued them over what they deemed was a violation of religious liberty. We understood the complexity and made clear this wasn't a matter of orthodoxy for us. We prayerfully supported our friends who made decisions that differed from ours.

What was most perplexing to me about this particular email, though, was that the congregant wasn't reacting against theologically questionable teaching, a moral failure, or an ethical violation. Instead, we were being accused of perpetrating evil by postponing gatherings during a pandemic.

A while back, a close friend who also serves as a pastor in town texted me, "Smart people are losing their minds." I haven't been able to shake that thought. Sometimes I find myself wondering, "Is it just me? Am I missing something? Am I the one losing my mind?" Maybe I am. But I think something more communally destructive is unfolding. It's not just me. It's *us*.

What we see happening in us is the result, in part, of deep cultural shifts. In the last three centuries, as the Enlightenment and the Industrial Revolution gave rise to modernity and eventually to postmodernity, the modern Western world has shifted to an era of *expressive individualism*, a phrase first coined by sociologist Robert Bellah and his coauthors in the 1985 book *Habits of the Heart*. Expressive individualism, "in its purest form, takes the individual, atomized self to be the fundamental unit of human reality. This self is not defined by its attachments or network of relations, but rather by its capacity to choose a future pathway that is revealed by the investigation of its own inner depths of sentiment."[1] This is our world. Infringing on the rights, privileges, desires, and longings of individuals is deemed a violent atrocity. This is not a liberal or conservative reality; it is a modern Western reality.

As such, concepts like *authority* and *communal responsibility* have been replaced by values like *autonomy* and *individual rights* taken to their extremes. This is why a Christian, when asked to worship remotely due to a public health crisis, can feel not only that their personal autonomy has been violated but also that it is the work of the devil itself. That's how deep our individualism runs.

We're here in large part because of the powerful tides of modernity and postmodernity that have been rising for hundreds of years. But we're here also because in the twenty-first century, the void left in our communities from our turn to individualism has been filled by an age-old phenomenon newly adrenalized by social media and the twenty-four-hour news cycle: the personality.

INTO THE VOID STEPS THE PERSONALITY

Every American born before the late 1990s remembers where they were on the morning of September 11, 2001. I was a college student late for class, rubbing the sleep from my eyes and plodding my way through the typical morning routine. I turned on the television as I brushed my teeth. Peter Jennings, the news anchor, was pale and looked more aged than usual. The reason unfolded quickly. I watched in disbelief. Paralyzed, I choked on the burn of toothpaste down my throat. After rinsing, I settled into the couch for what would become one of the most surreal days of my life, and all our lives.

At the time, the majority of Americans still relied on and trusted three major broadcast news networks. Though cable news was on the rise, ABC, NBC, and CBS made up the big three of televised journalism. Peter Jennings, Tom Brokaw, and Dan Rather were the faces and voices we knew and believed. As author Garrett Graff notes, "They were the closest that America had to national leaders on 9/11. They were the moral authority for the country on that first day."[2] In my early twenties at the time, as I watched and listened to these familiar faces explain the scene unfolding on my screen, I had no doubt that they were telling the truth. But I wonder how many twentysomethings would feel the same way today.

Societal distrust has been on the rise. Half of all Americans believe that fake news is a significant problem in our country[3] and that it is the responsibility of journalists to clean up the mess. But more than half of Americans also believe that journalists do not act in the best interest of the public.[4] So, there is decreasing trust in journalism and the expectation that journalism must fix the problem, but there is no trust in journalism to do so. This is our contemporary predicament.

Additionally, the development of artificial intelligence and its increasing presence in the digital world is amplifying the problem. In the summer of 2022, Jason Allen won first place in the Colorado State Fair art competition with a piece titled *Théâtre D'opéra Spatial*, which he created not with a brush and paint but using an AI platform called Midjourney. The backlash was fierce.

In the fall of that year, the popular comedian Joe Rogan released an episode of his long-format podcast called *The Joe Rogan Experience*, in which he interviews Steve Jobs. The only problem was that Jobs died in 2011, the interview never happened, and the voices heard weren't actually Rogan or Jobs but digitally generated copies, created by Podcast.ai, yet another AI platform growing in popularity.

In March 2023, Aza Raskin, co-founder of the Center for Humane Technology, signed up on Snapchat under a fake profile, pretending to be a thirteen-year-old girl. Snapchat had recently added an artificial intelligence bot to its platform, and Raskin proceeded to chat with the AI bot, letting it know that "she" had met a thirty-one-year-old man and was planning a secret "romantic getaway out of state." The bot proceeded to give the "girl" ideas on how to make the trip memorable by "setting the mood with candles or music."[5]

We were already struggling to trust what the talking heads were saying. Now we're faced with the problem of who the talking heads actually are and aren't and the potential dangers of their influence not only on adults but also on children. "Are they telling the truth?" has devolved into "Are they true?" and "What are their intentions?"

The writer and professor Jon Askonas reminds us that "a shared sense of reality is not natural. It is the product of social institutions that were once so powerful they could hold together a shared picture of the world."[6] But in the digital age, the media—news and social—has taken the place of social institutions, and our attention has become its most cherished commodity. And because the media has found that divisive content, whether false narratives, fake news, or emotionally charged clickbait, is the most effective way to keep us clicking, this new social institution is incentivized to actually work against our shared picture of the world. Our fracturing is the fuel that keeps the machine running. As a result, we find ourselves reeling.

In 1981, a political scientist from Harvard named Samuel Huntington wrote a book called *American Politics*. The subtitle is telling: *Promise of Disharmony*. Huntington suggests that every sixty years or so, American society and culture are upended by a surging uprising of what he calls "creedal passion," his term for describing a widespread "distrust of organized power."[7]

The Revolutionary period of the 1770s was a clear and obvious example of this, and every fifty to seventy-five years since, Huntington suggests that there have been similar society- and culture-wide uprisings, from the Jacksonian uprising of the 1820s, to the Progressive Era that began in the 1890s, to the social protest movements of the 1960s. And now the societal devastation of the 2020s.[8]

These uprisings, also called "moral convulsions" by Huntington, are marked by an overwhelming disgust people feel toward the general state of affairs, deep contempt toward established institutions of power or authority, increasing skepticism toward said institutions, and once fringe groups, generally made up of younger, emerging generations, seizing power through new modes of communication. I've not heard a more accurate and vivid description of the social media and twenty-four-hour-news-cycle age.

Into the void steps the *personality*. It's fair enough to say that media figures with public platforms have long been regarded as "personalities," but the degradation of journalistic integrity and widespread mistrust in anything institutional has led to a seismic shift in the sort of personalities rising to prominence today.

As a young child, I was a devoted fan of professional wrestling. I have vivid memories of Hulk Hogan wrestling "Macho Man" Randy Savage at Wrestlemania V in 1989. There was an entire year of buildup before the match: the two rivals formed an unlikely alliance, only for it to implode, leading to their championship grudge match at wrestling's premiere event. As a ten-year-old, I didn't know it was all scripted. I believed there was real hatred between these two men and that their match would unfold as a genuine athletic contest. But in reality, Terry "Hulk Hogan" Bollea and Randall "Macho Man" Poffo were actors—personalities—playing parts in a choreographed dance of madness and mayhem.

The former wrestling producer Eric Bischoff writes that although professional wrestling looks "like a staged, choreographed fight between two people who supposedly have an issue, something that they're fighting over…what you really don't see is the skill and the art that's required to engage the third person in that ring. The third person in the ring is the audience."[9]

The culture of public personalities today has much more in common with professional wrestling than with previous generations' iterations of media and journalism. In the modern-day wrestling ring of news and social media, there are heels and heroes, good guys and bad guys, playing parts and putting on performances, and we, the audience, are the third person in the ring.

As the personalities rage on, we are violently thrust back and forth against the ropes, clotheslines to the neck and elbows from the top rope. The noise of panic mongering overruns our feeds, and we find ourselves being thrashed about, flung from one side of any given cultural moment to the other. We end up beaten and battered. We need relief. Something steady and sure. Something anchored. Something timeless. We need what the Bible calls *everlasting*.

EL OLAM IN THE LAND OF THE PHILISTINES

In Genesis 21, we find an obscure story about Abraham making a covenant agreement with the Philistine king Abimelech, that he might dwell safely in the land of the Philistines with his family. The story tells us that "Abraham planted a tamarisk tree in Beersheba and called there on the name of *the Lord, the everlasting God*" (Genesis 21:33 ESV, emphasis added).

The Lord, the everlasting God.

Yahweh El Olam.

The placement of this story and Abraham's acknowledgment of God's eternal quality are important and, I believe, intentional. In an earlier part of Genesis 21, Abraham's wife, Sarah, gives birth to their first son, Isaac. This was the child God had promised them years earlier, and his birth was a miracle. Abraham was one hundred years old, Sarah ninety.

The story makes clear that God has a unique plan for this family and for this son in particular.

Then in Genesis 22, God asks Abraham to sacrifice this son who'd been gifted to them. In fact, the one story flows directly into the next.

> And Abraham sojourned many days in the land of the Philistines. After these things God tested Abraham and said to him, "Abraham!" And he said, "Here I am." He said, "Take your son, your only son Isaac, whom you love, and go to the land of Moriah, and offer him there as a burnt offering on one of the mountains of which I shall tell you." (Genesis 21:34–22:2 ESV)

El Olam, the Everlasting God, promises Abraham and Sarah a child.

Then, El Olam, the Everlasting God, asks Abraham to kill the child.

Abraham experiences the highest high and the lowest low that one can in life—the birth of a long-awaited child and the possible death of that beloved child—within the span of two chapters. And right in the middle of that story, Abraham calls on the name of the Everlasting God.

The gift of life.

Everlasting God.

The sacrifice of life.

This is Genesis 21–22.

Now, going back to the covenant for a moment, Abimelech isn't a personal name; it's a generic title given to all Philistine kings in the Old Testament, from the time of Abraham all the way through to the time of King David. So while God has a specific, unique name, the Philistine is given a generic name, akin to simply saying, "the Philistine king," or "you know, *that* guy, who was sort of like all the other guys."

Earthly kings come and go.

God is everlasting.

This too is Genesis 21–22.

Once more, back to the story. The word *sojourned*, used in Genesis 21:34, is a Hebrew word specifically meaning "to dwell as a foreigner or alien." Abraham dwells as an outsider in the land of the Philistines, where earthly kings come and go, vanquishing their enemies and flaunting their dominance. Despite the volatility, despite the instability, the everlasting God is with him.

As the people of God today, navigating a landscape laid waste by the calculated rage of personalities—seeming "kings"—we are sojourners through the land of the Philistines. We sense that we don't belong here. And in one sense, we don't. This isn't the world God intended.

But Abraham planted a tamarisk tree as a marker and reminder, before calling on the name of El Olam, the Everlasting God. Theologian Tremper Longman notes that "his planting of the tamarisk tree is a gesture that indicates he will be in the area for a while and that he belongs there."[10] Like

Abraham, we plant trees in the land of the modern-day Philistines because we too belong here in a strange, God-ordained way. We plant fruit-bearing trees that will grow slowly and steadily over time in a land torn apart by rage.

We do this in confident hope that while the present is veiled in a faux urgency, the truth is that God is eternal and timeless. We remember the words of the apostle Peter and the psalmist:

> But do not forget this one thing, dear friends: With the Lord a day is like a thousand years, and a thousand years are like a day. The Lord is not slow in keeping his promise, as some understand slowness. Instead he is patient with you, not wanting anyone to perish, but everyone to come to repentance. (2 Peter 3:8–9)

> Lord, you have been our dwelling place throughout all generations. Before the mountains were born or you brought forth the whole world, from everlasting to everlasting you are God...A thousand years in your sight are like a day that has just gone by, or like a watch in the night. (Psalm 90:1–2, 4)

Mathematics tells us that a day in this world is twenty-four hours, nothing more and nothing less. But time in God's kingdom works differently. This is one of the reasons why time's relentless and unstoppable march grows increasingly frustrating, even suffocating, as we age—because God has "set eternity in the human heart" (Ecclesiastes 3:11). In our angst, followers of Jesus also find relief from the rage by remembering that eternity is the way.

THE FUTURE IS COMING

I remember one night in March 2020, lying in bed, wide awake, doomscrolling Twitter. The COVID-19 pandemic had just broken out, and we were getting ready for lockdown. In the very early hours of the morning, I found myself in a panic. This is rare for me. But the glowing screen of my phone was telling me that we were now in a dystopia. I got in my car, drove to a grocery store several miles away, and bought as much toilet paper, canned goods, and water as they'd allow. It was something like two o'clock in the morning, and there were long lines in the store. I wasn't alone.

Eugene Peterson once wrote, "The way we conceive the future scripts the present, gives contour and tone to nearly every action and thought through the day... The Christian faith has always been characterized by a strong and focused sense of future... The practical effect of this belief is to charge each moment of the present with hope."[11] In that early-morning hour, I found myself, along with so many others, standing in line with a full shopping cart because at that moment we conceived the future a particular way.

This is not to downplay the need to plan and prepare. Planning and preparation are needed, of course. But there is

a particular way that God's people do this. We prepare and
plan in order to surrender our meager efforts into the capable
hands of a God who isn't confined by human limitations or
the limitations of time and space. The people of God dream
big, plan responsibly, and then offer all their plans back to
God—in that order. This sort of surrender is challenging for
a number of reasons, not the least of which is the prevailing
myth of human progress.

As recently as the beginning of the twentieth century,
the average global life expectancy was about thirty years and
even in the wealthiest nations, that number hovered around
fifty years. Two hundred years ago, the average global annual
income was about us$1,200.[12] Progress has undeniably been
made. This is something to appreciate and even celebrate, but
one of the consequences of this progress is that we've come to
believe that human flourishing is achieved solely by human
intellect, effort, and creativity.

Because things have gotten "better" in some ways, it's
easy even for Christians to forget that "many are the plans
in a person's heart, but it is the Lord's purpose that prevails"
(Proverbs 19:21). It is only when we commit whatever we do
to the Lord that he will establish our plans (Proverbs 16:3).
Professor and author Christopher Watkin astutely describes
the state of things this way:

The key move in transitioning from a biblical eschatology to the modern ideology of progress was the

substitution of human mastery for God's action. In Revelation, it is God and God alone who brings about the end: only the Lion of the tribe of Judah can open the seven seals; only God decides when the end will come. For modernity, humanity is in the driving seat: it is human effort, ingenuity, virtue, and labor that keep history rolling on towards perfection.[13]

As Watkin reminds us, a biblical eschatology is key. Eschatology is in essence the study of last things. It's commonly referred to within Christian theology as the "end times." Without a clear understanding of what the Bible tells us about how the human story ends (and then begins anew), it's easy for us to develop a dependence upon "human mastery," which will lead inevitably to disappointment. All things fall apart. As Patrick Deneen reminds us, "Among the greatest challenges facing humanity is the ability to survive progress."[14]

So what exactly does the Bible tell us about the end? There are plenty of places we can go in Scripture to explore this question, but the apostle Paul's first letter to the Thessalonian Christians is a great place to start.

The letter we call 1 Thessalonians today was written around AD 50, within two decades of Jesus' death, resurrection, and ascension, making it very likely the earliest New Testament document. Paul had planted the church in the city during his second missionary journey about one year earlier.

Thessalonica was an economically, culturally, and politically significant city. The Via Egnatia, a major road connecting the eastern regions of the Roman Empire to the capital, ran straight through Thessalonica, drawing around two hundred thousand residents to the city. It was also a highly polytheistic city, full of idols of a wide variety of deities. As a port city on the Aegean Sea, Thessalonica offered on a clear day a view of Mount Olympus across the water. At the time, Mount Olympus was considered to be the home of the gods, the epicenter of divine activity in the ancient Greco-Roman world. The early Christians in Thessalonica lived quite literally in the shadow of false gods with their false promises of the world to come.

These false gods were in many ways the personalities of the first-century world. Their cultural influence loomed large, amplified by the pagan religious leaders of the day. And in this context, Paul writes to the followers of Jesus in Thessalonica, reminding them throughout his letter of how the true story of humanity would end (and begin anew).

What is our hope, our joy, or the crown in which we will glory in the presence of our Lord Jesus when he *comes*? (1 Thessalonians 2:19, emphasis added)

May he strengthen your hearts so that you will be blameless and holy in the presence of our God and Father when our Lord Jesus *comes*. (1 Thessalonians 3:13, emphasis added)

For the Lord himself will *come* down from heaven, with a loud command, with the voice of the archangel and with the trumpet call of God. (1 Thessalonians 4:16, emphasis added)

May your whole spirit, soul and body be kept blameless at the *coming* of our Lord Jesus Christ. (1 Thessalonians 5:23, emphasis added)

The Greek word translated into the English as *come* or *coming* is *parousia*. At the time, the word was laced with deep religious and political associations. In religious life, for example, *parousia* was an expression for the arrival or revealing of a deity. In civic life and politics, *parousia* was the official term for the arrival of any visiting person of high rank, especially kings and emperors.

There was a cult in Thessalonica dedicated to a pagan god named Dionysus; he was commonly referred to as "the god of epiphany" or "the god who arrives," and a common phrase in Thessalonica was "the *parousia* of Dionysus." When the Thessalonian Christians heard about the *parousia* of Jesus, they would have heard it, in their context, as Paul intended—as a rebuke of the "coming" or "arrival" of false gods.

This was a critically important part of Paul's message to the early church. Because the culture was filled with false gods offering false promises, the first followers of Jesus needed to be reminded time and again that their resurrected and ascended Lord would someday return, coming to right all wrongs and restore all things. Without this long view, Paul believed that the urgency of the present would pull Christians away from the one true God to false personalities.

Similarly, the personalities of our day understand that our fear and angst can easily be exploited. It's not in their interest to offer a message of peace or hope. They need us to click, swipe, share, and retweet feverishly.

Keep us anxious. Keep attuned. That's the formula.

It isn't so much that the rage of personalities is completely unwarranted. Sometimes it is. The world's gone mad and life's a mess. Many of us feel this way, much and maybe most of the time. But the knowledge of the coming of Christ settles us down by reminding us, in the words of John Ortberg, "There will be great pain, and there will be great joy. In the end, joy wins. So if joy has not yet won, it is not yet the end."[15] It is not yet the end.

And we know how the story ends. The anxious frenzy will give way to the arrival of our returned Lord and can give way even now to his presence. And thus we find relief beneath the long shadow of Christ's future coming, a relief that is truly found in Paul's exhortation toward the end of his first letter to the Thessalonians, "Pray without ceasing" (5:17 ESV).

PRAYER AND THE TIMELESS VOICE OF GOD

I have a book that sits on my desk called *A Diary of Daily Prayer* by a twentieth-century Scottish pastor named John

Baille. The opening lines of the book read: "Eternal Father of my soul, let my first thought today be of you, let my first impulse be to worship you, let my first word be your Name, let my first action be to kneel before you in prayer."[16]

Over the years these few lines have helped me navigate countless struggles, offering a practical approach to prayer by giving us four key invitations to step into each day:

"Let my first thought today be of you."
"Let my first impulse be to worship you."
"Let my first word be your Name."
"Let my first action be to kneel before you in prayer."

Although *prayer* is the last word in the last line, in my estimation and experience, all four points are collectively an invitation to prayer. The late pastor and author Tim Keller talked about prayer being a pilgrimage, noting that "To be in pilgrimage is to have not yet arrived. There is a longing in prayer that is never fulfilled in this life, and sometimes the deep satisfactions we are looking for in prayer feel few and far between. Prayer is a journey."[17] The journey begins with our thoughts and impulses, the ideas and desires that begin to orient the direction of our days and, in turn, the direction of our lives. This leads then to our words and actions, what we speak into the world.

For many of us, as we engage our world and the

personality-driven media specifically, the cycle looks something like this:

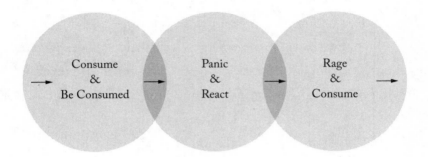

As we consume content more and more, the content eventually consumes us. We're flooded with thoughts and feelings, leading to panic, and in a desperate attempt to alleviate the tension, we react, often in rage. We ourselves contribute to the cacophony and chaos, leading us right back to where we started, consuming more of the same.

But the pilgrimage of prayer leads us down a far more sane and sustainable path. Paul's invitation to "pray without ceasing" (1 Thessalonians 5:17 ESV) marks the trail. It isn't so much about verbalizing prayers at all times, which would be near impossible. As the theologian J. B. Lightfoot notes, "It is not in the moving of the lips, but in the elevation of the heart to God, that the essence of prayer consists."[18] While the world rages on, followers of Jesus can find calm by elevating our hearts to God, without ceasing.

Prayer slows us down enough to thoughtfully observe rather than frantically consume. As we lift our hearts to

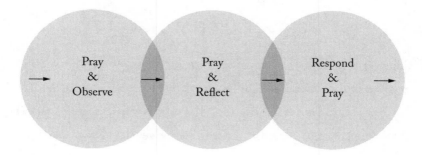

God, we remind ourselves that our story has already been written. What's happening today matters, but what happened two thousand years ago and what will happen on the day of Christ's return are the chapters that matter most. Prayer settles us into that great truth. As such, we don't consume nor are we consumed by the rage of the day; we view it at an appropriate distance. We continue to pray and reflect, surrendering our impulses to the Lord. We respond as needed, but always with gentleness, grace, humility, care, confidence in who's really in charge of the world, and more prayer.

As creatures bound by time, we who dare to listen to the timeless voice of God through prayer are climbers venturing off on an expedition, away from all the clamor and rage. Sometimes, the climb is a slog, a struggle up a steep mountain. Most days it seems easier to stay at base camp and resign ourselves to the noise of our day. But doing so means missing out on the breathtaking quiet and clarity of a life above and away from the personalities, talking heads, and divisiveness stealing our attention.

FURTHER UP, FURTHER IN

Denver is known as the mile-high city, but what many don't realize is that Colorado Springs, about ninety minutes south, is seven hundred feet higher. The air is thin, and physical exertion there, especially for a lifetime sea-level guy like me, is felt in the body in shocking ways. So, of course, a couple of years ago when some friends invited me to hike the Manitou Incline, I said yes.

The Manitou Incline is an extreme hike near Colorado Springs. The average grade is 45 percent and gets as steep as 68 percent. If those numbers don't mean anything to you, that's okay. It's steep. At certain points, the hike feels far more like climbing a ladder than climbing steps. The base of the hike sits at about 6,500 feet elevation, where the air is already thin. The peak sits at 8,600 feet elevation, which is about 1.6 miles above sea level. It's so high you can see Kansas, 150 miles away.

The hike took me two hours. Multiple times I contemplated heading back. My lungs burned and my legs felt heavy. But my friends wouldn't let me stop. And I wouldn't let them stop. We pushed and encouraged each other, "spurring one another on" in the words of the writer of Hebrews (10:24). The Greek for *spur* is *paroxysmon*, which can mean both "encouragement" and "disagreement" or "intense arguing." It's a fascinating word.

This is what prayer often feels like to me, an honest and often raw dialogue with God, full of the normal highs, lows, and long plateaus we experience in any meaningful relationship. And I know I'm not alone. You've felt this way in prayer too. Sometimes prayer is a dance, fluid and free. Often prayer is a wrestling match, tense and taut. But the journey is always worth it.

In our exhaustion and weariness from all the noise, prayer in all its forms sustains us. Tim Keller once wrote that prayer is "a kind of travelers' waybread . . . [it] helps us endure."[19]

Prayer helps us endure.

Many people have said to me over the years that they don't like praying publicly because they're "not good at it." They think they're not eloquent, inspiring, or theologically brilliant enough. But prayer isn't about excellence. No one looks good hiking up Manitou, not even the most experienced hikers. Everyone is sweating and beaten down, taking one step at a time, just like everyone else.

It isn't about excellence.

It's about endurance.

In the chaos and cacophony, prayer leads us to a settledness in God, in his timeless voice and the long story he's unfolding in the world. But the journey doesn't have to look, feel, or sound excellent. We just have to endure. So often when we go to prayer, we seek the mountaintop without the grueling climb up the steps.

Most days, my prayers are boring. They're wholly ordinary. But there's also magic in the mundane. The writer Tish Harrison Warren reminds us that "all these boring parts matter to God," and the stuff that feels "small and insignificant to us are weighty with meaning and part of the abundant life God has for us."[20] "How I spend this ordinary day in Christ," she adds, "is how I will spend my Christian life."[21]

Prayer is rarely loud, like the personalities who conquer our feeds.

It is mostly ordinary, mostly mundane, mostly slow.

But it is also the means by which we hear the timeless voice of God in the present.

In prayer, El Olam, our everlasting God, meets us in the now.

The personalities of our day play tricks with their rage.

But prayer guides us toward true magic.

In *The Last Battle*, C. S. Lewis's conclusion to his classic Chronicles of Narnia series, after the war has been won and all has been set right, the unicorn Jewel speaks these indelible words: "I have come home at last! This is my real country! I belong here. This is the land I have been looking for all my life, though I never knew it till now. The reason why we loved the old Narnia is that it sometimes looked a little like this. Bree-hee-hee! Come further up, come further in!"[22]

He'd arrived in his home country, his final place, at peace and at rest. Yet still, there was still further up, further in to go. Amid all the clamor and outrage, may we remember that there is still further up and further in to go.

What is will not always be.

What is not yet will someday be.

And God, in his everlasting, timeless love, brings to bear now, today, here, what will someday be.

Eternity is available today.

And we have no reason to fear, no reason to be anxious, no reason to rage.

Further up. Further in. One step at a time.

Two

God's Daily Voice amid the Predictions of Pundits

Uncertainty is uncomfortable. All of us would prefer a knowable future over an unpredictable one. So we pay close attention to those who are confident in telling us not only how things are but how things will be. Despite widespread skepticism toward the news media, we still lend our ears to the pundits.

In 2016, a political analyst named Sam Wang predicted the presidential election for Hillary Clinton. This wasn't news. All the pundits were predicting that Donald Trump would lose in a landslide. Polls gave Clinton anywhere between a 70 percent and, in some cases, as high as a 99 percent chance to win the presidency.[1] What made Wang stand out was a public bet he made—if Trump won the election Wang would eat a live insect. Shortly after election night, Sam Wang ate a cricket live on CNN.[2] Wang is a brilliant man. He teaches neuroscience at Princeton University and founded a popular blog on data-based political predictions. But he was wrong. The pundit predicted incorrectly. And he ate a bug for it.

Over the course of several years in the 1950s, when South Africa was in the early days of apartheid, a university professor named Kurt Danziger surveyed hundreds of South African high school and college students, asking them to predict what might unfold in their country for the remainder of the century. The instructions were clear: "This is not a test of imagination—just describe what you really expect to happen."[3] Nearly 70 percent of Black and 80 percent of Indian South Africans, two people groups most adversely affected by racial segregation, predicted the end of apartheid. Only 4 percent of white South Africans, those benefiting most, predicted the same.

Danzinger concluded that "those who were the beneficiaries of the existing state of affairs were extremely reluctant to predict its end, while those who felt oppressed by the same situation found it all too easy to foresee its collapse."[4] Predictions are not objective.

Research has shown that most predictions, no matter how unbiased the individual believes them to be, are skewed toward personally preferred outcomes. Noting that predictions are much more like wish-fulfillment fantasies than we might think, one researcher explains that people "seek to achieve greater cognitive simplicity by treating probability and desirability as a single dimension."[5] And yet, despite the biased and inherently volatile nature of predictions, we are drawn to them anyway. Why? Because we want our desires to become reality, and we need to believe that they will.

In 1982, the futurist (and first female nominee for vice president, in 1984) Barbara Hubbard predicted in the *New York Times* that in twenty years, humans would "cultivate the stars" and that there was the distinct possibility of "a cosmic civilization" by the early 2000s.[6] But here we are, well into the 2020s, and not a single person has a house on the moon (though by the time this book makes it into your hands, maybe Elon Musk has broken ground on the dark side). Where did this prediction come from? Hubbard was a brilliant woman, and yes, some of her thinking was based on data. But she also belonged to a group of thinkers in the 1970s who were working on a proposal to establish a lunar colony, intended as a sort of renewed utopia in space. In other words, Hubbard's prediction was in fact an extension of her desires.

This is why students living in the same country at the same time can predict such drastically different futures, even when asked to do so objectively. This is why brilliant analysts end up eating insects on television. This is why the entire concept of punditry is not what we think.

The word *pundit* originally referred to religious leaders and advisors to kings. Etymologically, the word derives from the Sanskrit word *pandita*, which means "a learned man or scholar." The word first shows up in the English language in the late seventeenth century, in references to court officials in colonial India who gave counsel to British officials regarding Hindu law.

When Britain colonized India in the 1800s, government

officials paid locals to help them survey the land, to act as guides across unknown and unfamiliar terrain. These guides were called pundits. This is how we often think of pundits today, as guides helping us navigate the unfamiliar terrain of the future, with foreknowledge and expertise. This is why we tune in to our news network of choice during election season, with the digital map of America displayed in all of its glory— states going from red to blue and back to red and then back to blue, electoral votes and popular votes rising and falling. We watch and wait with bated breath as the enlightened professionals tell us what will happen.

We listen. We believe. Then, disappointment.

In some ways, it doesn't matter how accurate a pundit's projections might be. A media talking head might correctly predict the next president, and that next president may very well be our candidate of choice. But the guarantee of disappointment looms large. Pundits and presidents will inevitably let us down. They will not lead us, totally and completely, to the truly "good life" we were promised during the campaign. Expectations always outpace outcomes, in politics and in life. But we continue to hold out hope that the future will be better than the present and that *when* that future arrives, all will be well.

When the economy turns around...

When the pandemic ends...

When the law gets overturned...

When I get that promotion...
When I find that spouse...
When I finally move...

And because our hopes are fixed on these desired futures, we gravitate toward the pundits who tell us this is where things are headed and who affirm our vision for tomorrow. Again, we need our desires to become reality and we need to believe that they will. So we look to the media who will tell us what we want to hear.

But this sort of obsession with what *could be* leads to an utterly anxious life in the midst of what actually *is*. Steve Cuss puts it this way: "The story we tell ourselves infects reality and shapes what actually 'is' and turns it into what we think 'is.' God is on the other side of what we think 'is,' which is why we access so much power and freedom if we can move beyond the stories we tell ourselves."[7]

God is on the other side of what we think *is*.

But the other side is not some far-off distant place out there on the horizons of our desired futures. The other side is actually right here.

While pundits carry on about what *might be*, God is ever present in what truly *is*.

While we fixate on what the future holds, God holds the future and draws near to us in the here and now.

While we dream of milk and honey in the Promised Land, God offers us daily bread.

WHAT IS IT?

Aleksander Gamme is a Norwegian adventurer and explorer. He's climbed Mount Everest, biked across the Sahara Desert, and in 2011 he completed the first solo hike across Antarctica. The hike took Gamme eighty-seven days. He carried minimal food and supplies in order to lighten his load, and as part of that strategy, throughout the front leg of his journey, Gamme buried snacks in the snow, marking his hidden treasures with bright flags, so that he'd have food awaiting him on the back leg of the trek.

On day eighty-six, Gamme came across one of his last stashes. At this point, exhausted and nearing a breaking point, he had no recollection of what exactly he'd buried in the snow, only that it was some form of sustenance. But on this day, he decided to film himself on his phone. Very shortly after posting the video online,[8] it went viral.

It's almost impossible to watch the video without breaking out into an unforced grin. Gamme begins with anticipation and desperation as he urgently digs into the snow. Eventually, he discovers a bag of Cheez Doodles, a box of crackers, and some candy. In total, it was probably less than ten dollars' worth of "food" one would purchase at a gas station. But for Gamme, starving and shivering his way across the tundra, it might as well have been a tasting menu with wine pairings at The French Laundry.

At one point, after uncontrolled fits of laughter and primal screams of joy, Gamme lies on his back and begins singing "Hallelujah." Gamme is not a religious man. But in this incredible moment of relief, he finds himself uttering sacred words.

Hallelujah.

Hallel Yah.

Praise Yahweh.

Gamme's Cheez Doodles remind me of the manna from heaven in the Exodus story. Shortly after God had delivered the Israelites from slavery and rescued them from the armies of Pharaoh, the people of God find themselves wandering the desert on their way to the Promised Land. In Exodus 15, after God parted the Red Sea and the people crossed to safety on dry land, they sang, "In your unfailing love you will lead the people you have redeemed. In your strength you will guide them to your holy dwelling" (v. 13). Then, just one chapter later, "the whole community grumbled against Moses and Aaron" (Exodus 16:2).

Two short months after God had broken through four centuries of enslavement, because of physical hunger and emotional anxiety, the people of God exclaim, "If only we had died by the Lord's hand in Egypt! There we sat around pots of meat and ate all the food we wanted, but you have brought us out into the desert to starve this entire assembly to death" (Exodus 16:3). They'd so quickly forgotten that in Egypt, they were slaves, laboring to make bricks for an empire that saw them as tools rather than humans.

Two short months into their salvation, the people of God forgot the reality of the past—where they'd been and what God had done—and forged a narrative about the future, that they'd starve to death in the desert.

Two short months into their salvation, gratitude had turned to grumbling. In our day, gratitude often devolves into grumbling because our need to know the future in order to protect our present always shortens the path to grumbling.

There is a difference between praying toward the future and fixating on the future. Fixation is a form of control. But praying toward the future is a way of asking God to align our will and desire with his. It is a means of surrender.

I often pray for my two young children. Like any loving parent, I want the absolute best for them and sometimes worry that the challenges before them are too great. But praying for them is ultimately a way of surrendering them. It's a way of acknowledging that God loves them far more than I ever could and that outcomes are not mine to control.

Because of their present hunger, the Israelites could no longer see with clarity that their journey was toward the promised land, and instead, they clamored for their past life. This is what uncertainty in the wildernesses of life can do to us. Because the future seems uncertain and we find ourselves desperate for a clear path forward in the present, the path of least resistance often seems to be what we've already known.

But despite the people's forgetfulness about the past and fear about the future, God moves among them in the present.

He rains bread from heaven called manna, which literally translates to "What is it?" A mysterious and (literally) heavenly carb to sustain the people in the wilderness. This unexpected gift sustains the people in their anxiety and uncertainty. No one could have predicted this. It was God's way of showing up to provide, inviting his people to show up in return to receive, every single day.

GIVE US TODAY

Harkening back to this surprising story of manna in the wilderness, Jesus teaches his followers to pray, "Give us today our *daily* bread" (Matthew 6:11, emphasis added).

On the surface, this prayer seems simple enough. It's a petition for God to provide for our needs. But there's much more here than initially meets the eye. The word translated as "daily" is the Greek word *epiousios*, and its exact meaning is somewhat debated. It could mean "needed," "current," "tomorrow," or "the coming day." What's clear, though, is that the prayer is not:

Give us today our *annual* bread.

Give us today our *long-term* bread.

Give us today our *retirement* bread.

"Give us today our daily bread" is a way of praying, "Teach us to *daily* rely on you," or "Teach us to rely on you *today*. Then *tomorrow*. Then *the day after that* too."

This sort of daily dependence on God is a challenge for

most of us, not because it isn't necessary or true but because the comforts of life in the modern world tend to minimize or obliterate our awareness of just how dependent we are.

When my daughter was born, the doctors found a small hole in her heart. They told us that monitoring it was of utmost importance. Heart surgery was a possibility. We ran some tests and waited a couple of weeks for definitive results. During that time, on most nights when I held my little girl to rock her to sleep, I prayed while fighting back tears. The sobering reality of her fragility weighed heavily on me, and there was nothing I could do but surrender her life to God, who I had to believe was with us each day, amid our uncertainty and fear of the next. I was reminded that each breath she and I breathed together was a gift.

"The Spirit of God has made me; the breath of the Almighty gives me life." (Job 33:4)

In him we live and move and have our being. (Acts 17:28)

While the world lives on the precipice of the present, overlooking a future we long to see but can't ever know for sure, followers of Jesus are taught to pray for *daily bread*. Followers of Jesus trust that tomorrow, there will be another portion of God's provision to sustain us. And in so doing, the Christian is able to live most fully in the present, confident that though we do not know what the future holds, we know who holds the future, and there is nothing to fear.

THE GOD WHO IS (EVERYW)HERE

Recently I took my family for the first time to Joshua Tree National Park. Staring out across the vastness, enveloped by ancient rocks and an endless horizon, one feels utterly small— tiny, really. And yet, simultaneously, I felt so incredibly aware and alive. To think, the God who mustered the grandeur of such a place with but a word is here still, in this place, and in my life. It was astonishing.

In his classic book *The Knowledge of the Holy*, A. W. Tozer writes, "The doctrine of omnipresence personalizes a man's relation to the universe in which he finds himself. This great central truth gives meaning to all truths and imparts supreme value to all his little life. God is present, near him, next to him, and this God sees him and knows him through and through."[9] Do you believe this? I don't mean just intellectually. Do you sense, in a very real way, that God is present, near you, next to you, that God knows you through and through? It is only in sensing the very real nearness of God that we're able to free ourselves from the paralyzing grip of unknown futures.

The psalmist writes:

Where can I go from your Spirit? Where can I flee from your presence? If I go up to the heavens, you are there; if I make my bed in the depths, you are there. If I rise on the wings of the dawn, if I settle on the far side of the sea, even there your hand will guide me, your right hand will hold me fast. If I say, "Surely the darkness will hide me and the light become night around me," even the darkness will not be dark to you; the night will shine like the day, for darkness is as light to you. (Psalm 139:7–12)

The Hebrew word for "Spirit" is *ruakh*, which means "breath" or "wind," similar in meaning to the Greek word for "Spirit," *pneuma*. The psalmist's question "Where can I go from your Spirit?" is rhetorical and, in some ways, intentionally absurd. The answer is obviously nowhere, for the very breath in our lungs is a reminder of the Spirit of God's nearness to his people—to us, with us, and in us.

Then, the psalmist asks a second question: "Where can I flee from your presence?" The Hebrew word for "presence" is *panyim*, meaning "face," "in front of," or "in the sight of." Wherever we go and whatever we're going through, there is no place where God does not see us. We are always in his line of sight; even when we don't see him, he sees us. A bit more on that in the next chapter.

The point here is that even as our eyes wander ahead toward the uncertainty of the future and as our desperate, listening ears are taken hostage by the noisy punditry of so-called experts attempting to appease our fears with prognostications that amount to not much more than biased guesses, the God who knows all is as close as breath and he sees us even when we can't see him.

> Those who devise wicked schemes are near, but they are far from your law. Yet you are near, Lord, and all your commands are true. (Psalm 119:150–151)

> The Lord is near to all who call on him, to all who call on him in truth. (Psalm 145:18)

> The Lord is close to the brokenhearted and saves those who are crushed in spirit. (Psalm 34:18)

> Draw near to God, and he will draw near to you. (James 4:8 NRSV)

A few years ago at an amusement park in Southern California featuring talking mice and an endless array of princesses adorned in brightly colored dresses, my son, just three at the time, wandered off for a moment to follow one of said mice. I had my eye on him the entire time, but at a certain point, he lost track of me. I could see his expression turn from joy to confusion to fear, and before he broke out in an all-out panic, I rushed over to him. He saw me among the crowd as I drew closer and immediately left the mouse to draw near to me, and all was well.

The pundits of our day offer solace for our fear and comfort for our anxiety by offering us a wide array of opinions, all just shots in the dark, subjective and skewed. They attempt to steady our instability by simply burying us beneath a mountain of predictions. But God offers us no such thing.

God does not predict, because he already knows.

God does not predict, because he has already seen.

God does not predict, because he has already done all that needs to be done.

God does not offer us a peek into the future.

God offers us only and all of himself in the here and now.

Daily bread for today. And tomorrow. And the day after that.

Because that's what good fathers do.

FISH OR SNAKE

Back to the Exodus story for a moment. As the Israelites grumble and complain, God says to Moses, "I will rain down bread from heaven for you. The people are to go out each day and gather enough for that day. In this way I will test them and see whether they will *follow* my *instructions*" (Exodus 16:4, emphasis added). Seems like a strange, maybe even exploitive, way to test people's loyalty. Keep them fed just enough and hungry just enough to test whether they'll keep obeying orders? Is that the sort of God he is?

In the original Hebrew, the word for "follow" is *yalach*, and it means something more along the lines of "going" or "walking toward." It's a word that indicates motion in a direction more so than a blind, static compliance in place. It's the word used when God instructs Abraham to leave his home country and "go" to the land God would show him (see Genesis 12:1) and to describe an obscure man named Enoch who "walked faithfully" with God for three hundred years (Genesis 5:22). *Yalach* is less about following orders in an instruction manual and more about obedience on the journey toward God, leading to a life of increasing nearness, and, as a result, increasing safety, security, and provision.

Now, this might be a bit confusing, because God does say, "I will test them and see whether they will follow my *instructions*" (Exodus 16:4, emphasis added). The Hebrew word for "instructions" is *Torah*, which is probably familiar to some. It's the word used specifically to describe the first five books of the Hebrew Scriptures, what many of us call the Old Testament, and it is found all over the Bible, more than two hundred times, in fact. The word is used more generally to describe God's directions and guidance for life, that his people might flourish and thrive. We see this especially throughout the Psalms.

The [*Torah*] of the Lord is perfect, refreshing the soul. (Psalm 19:7, emphasis added)

The [*Torah*] from your mouth is more precious to me
than thousands of pieces of silver and gold. (Psalm
119:72, emphasis added)

Your [*Torah*] gives me delight. (Psalm 119:174, emphasis added)

God provides manna from heaven, just enough for the day,
not primarily to test loyalties but to invite a daily closeness,
which leads to refreshing and delight.

God doesn't hold out on good things *from* his people. God
holds out his hand *toward* his people, his hand from which all
truly good things are offered.

Every good and perfect gift is from above, coming
down from the Father of the heavenly lights, who does
not change like shifting shadows. (James 1:17)

This is one of the dangerous myths of punditry in the
secular age. The twentieth-century philosopher Charles Taylor
wrote about what he called the "immanent frame." In short,
the immanent frame is the secular ideology, or what Taylor
calls social imaginary, that everything in the world is purely
material and physical. From this comes the predominant belief
in the modern West that there exists no reality outside of what
we can see, smell, taste, touch, and feel, and that reality is simply a complex system of causal relationships between material

matter and physical interactions. The immanent frame stands at odds with any sense or possibility of transcendence, anything that cannot be explained within the confines of the natural world. It has no category for the supernatural.

This has led us to the belief, even among Christians, that if something cannot be fixed through the natural order of things by humans, through human intellect and ingenuity, then it cannot be fixed at all. And hence our intense addiction to the noise of pundits today. They show us the path we must take toward crafting the world we long for, and declare for us whether we are on that path or not.

In light of this, many Christians today in the modern Western world are functional atheists. We sort of believe intellectually that God is powerful and in control and can do all things. But the lives we live, the way we prioritize our time and energy and passions, the way we fret and worry and agonize over outcomes we can't actually control tells a different story—the myth that we must make our own way because God either can't or won't or both.

Into this reality, Jesus asks, "Which of you fathers, if your son asks for a fish, will give him a snake instead? Or if he asks for an egg, will give him a scorpion? If you then, though you are evil, know how to give good gifts to your children, how much more will your Father in heaven give the Holy Spirit to those who ask him!" (Luke 11:11–13).

We want the fish but fear we'll get the snake. So we have to ask ourselves, *What sort of Father is he, really?* We have a Father who gives good things. He may not give them in the specific ways and within the specific times we long for. And they may not always look, sound, or feel like the gifts we expected or longed for. But they are gifts in the truest and greatest sense. Notice in the passage above that Jesus doesn't say "how much more will your Father in heaven give the things *you want* to those who ask him!" He says that to those who ask, the *Holy Spirit* will be given. His Spirit, which is himself, the very breath of our Trinitarian God, breathing life into us, sustaining and nourishing us, providing for our needs.

We lose sight of this incredible gift of God's available presence because our eyes are so often wandering the far horizons, searching for the extravagant and the extraordinary. But all the while, daily bread is right in front of us, beautifully and surprisingly offered most accessibly and consistently through ancient texts typically lying dormant and collecting dust on our shelves.

SCRIPTURE AND THE DAILY VOICE OF GOD

In middle school I received an allowance from my mother, like most kids. But unlike most kids, my allowance wasn't based on getting chores done but rather on memorizing Bible verses. She'd write a new verse on a small three-by-five-inch flashcard each week and have me read it over and over again on the drive to school every morning. While it was a mostly transactional exercise for me at the time, in hindsight, familiarity with the practice of putting Scripture to memory is something I'm immensely grateful for.

Wendell Berry writes that "To lose the scar of knowledge is to renew the wound."[10] In my experience, meaningful and consistent engagement with the Bible isn't so much about deepening my knowledge or elevating my spirituality as it is about running my finger over the scar of my own sin and brokenness, remembering again and again what it took to change my story and the human story, and, maybe most important, hearing God, the great author of that story, speaking day by day.

In the first book of the New Testament, one of the intentions of the author, Matthew, is to present Jesus as a new Moses, whose arrival marks the beginning of a new journey through the wilderness toward a land of promise. But unlike the original Exodus story, this Promised Land is not a physical location on the far side of the desert but is instead the kingdom of God itself, embodied in Jesus himself.

Early on in the story, Jesus fasts in the wilderness for forty days. This is a deliberate and intentional allusion to the hunger of the Israelites and God's provision of manna in the first story.

> Then Jesus was led by the Spirit into the wilderness to be tempted by the devil. After fasting forty days and forty nights, he was hungry. The tempter came to him and said, "If you are the Son of God, tell these stones

to become bread." Jesus answered, "It is written: 'Man shall not live on bread alone, but on every word that comes from the mouth of God.'" (Matthew 4:1–4)

The devil tempts Jesus to take matters into his own hands. "The solution is simple," he whispers. "You're hungry. Turn the stones into bread and hunger no more." But the lie is woven into the invitation deceptively, almost in disguise.

"If you are the Son of God," the devil says.

This isn't about Jesus satisfying his hunger.

This is about Jesus' identity and his relationship with the Father.

Would a good God allow a Son he loves to hunger?

If a good God would allow such a thing, he must be something less than good. Or, probably more likely, I must not be his beloved Son.

This is the devil's tactic.

We often get sucked into the chaos and cacophony of modern-day pundits because we've been deceived by similar lies.

Would a good God allow us to languish in such dire and desperate circumstances?

Jesus' response to the lie shows us the way through: "Man shall not live on bread alone, but on every word that comes from the mouth of God."

In short, this is a way of saying "Despite my temporary hunger, the truth about my identity has already been spoken.

I have the daily bread I need: every word that comes from the mouth of God."

So many of us find ourselves desperately hungry for hope, healing, and a way through the mess of our lives and the world—broken relationships, financial uncertainty, fear of the unknown, the bitter sting of disappointment after disappointment, on and on. And in our need, we've grown accustomed to feasting on a daily diet of news and social media punditry while merely nibbling at or completely ignoring the Scriptures.

But the Bible is the most accessible and available form of soul nourishment, daily bread, God offers us. It gives us an honest picture of the human condition—our desires, our hopes, and the trials that we'll all face—and, most important, shows us how to navigate through those trials. In this sense it offers hope. The Bible also gives us a picture of our Creator, who alone can satisfy our desires.

But indulgence and moderation have been misallocated in our lives. We feast on the news and dangerously moderate our intake of Scripture. This leads to a life consumed by the news and frustrated by Scripture, which requires deep, thoughtful, consistent engagement. This eventually and inevitably leaves us grumbling, anxious, and uncertain.

When, where, and even how we eat differs from household to household, individual to individual. But regularly consuming substantive, nourishing food is what matters. So it is with the daily bread of God's word. When we feast daily on the Word of God and moderate our news intake, we become

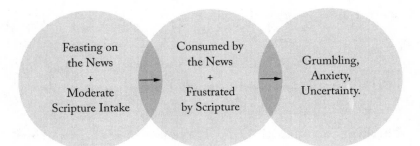

consumed by Scripture, and news takes its appropriate place as merely a means for informing us of current events, rather than holding formational power over us.

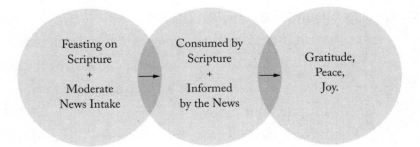

Feasting on Scripture leads to a life of gratitude, peace, and joy.

Gratitude, because it is a story of God's grace, leading us out of sin and brokenness and into life and life to the full.

Peace, because it is the story of God's justice, setting all wrong things right, in part today, in full on the day of Christ's return.

Joy, because it is the story of God's presence, with us at

all times in all things, sustaining and satisfying us in spite of circumstances and situations.

But what does feasting on Scripture look like?

We must remember that it's *daily* bread. I don't mean this to be legalistic. I just mean it as an undeniable part of human reality. Just as your body cannot go long without food, so your soul cannot go long without the Word. Sure, you can limp along but just as your body will not function at optimum capacity without eating consistently, so your soul will not function adequately without the Bible consistently.

This is what it looks like for me. Most mornings, I wake up around five a.m. I have young kids who are up by six thirty a.m., so any quiet time I need has to come early. I set up my drip coffee the night before, and in the darkness of early morning, I remind myself prayerfully of the gift of a home, water, electricity, and freshly ground coffee. As the water pours over the granules, I open my Bible. I read a Psalm or two, then am almost always someplace in the Gospels. The Psalms and the Gospels constitute my early-morning time dining on daily bread.

At our church we have yearlong cohorts called Discover the Bible. Groups of people get together and commit to reading the entire Bible in one year. The cohorts include an online platform to share thoughts, questions, and encouragement. Once a month, anyone who wants to can gather online for an hour-long question and response discussion with me or another one of our pastors on staff. So I try to keep up with their reading schedule as well.

Every few months, as the cohorts prepare to enter a new significant section of Scripture—the Pentateuch, the Prophets, the Wisdom writings, the Gospels, the Epistles, etc.—we offer labs, which are interactive learning environments that deep dive into the literary and historical context of major sections of biblical writing, to train and equip the cohorts to engage the upcoming section of Scripture with some helpful tools.

None of this is particularly noteworthy or novel. It's not easy but it's simple. But it's always the long and steady commitment to the simple stuff that forms us. I love the way Tish Harrison Warren puts it: "If I am to spend my whole life being transformed by the Good News of Jesus, I must learn how grand, sweeping truths—doctrine, theology, ecclesiology, Christology—rub against the texture of an average day. How I spend this ordinary day in Christ is how I will spend my Christian life."[11]

Daily bread isn't always exhilarating or exciting. On most days, as I read the Psalms or the Gospels, I'm tired. I've read the story of Jesus healing the blind man while rubbing the sleep from my own eyes. Almost always the entire thing is remarkably ordinary. My spirit doesn't stir, my soul doesn't warm, my heart doesn't beat out of my chest. It's mostly quiet and still and boring. Professor and author Karen Swallow Prior reminds us that "Practice makes perfect, but pleasure makes practice more likely, so read something enjoyable."[12] I wholeheartedly agree and would add that it's reciprocal; practice over time can actually make something enjoyable. Practice can create pleasure, which in turn creates a continued desire to practice, and so on.

I go back to the Scriptures, day after day, because over the course of months and years and now nearly two decades of relying on daily bread, I've come to genuinely enjoy it. My desires have been reformed. My appetite for the wild prognostications, projections, and punditry of our day has waned, and significantly so. I am comfortable not knowing—not with all things but with many things, maybe even most things. And one of the primary reasons for this is because I know how the story ends. I've read it and experienced and feasted on it for years. And I still do, every day. It is daily bread, after all.

Many years ago when I was a student ministries pastor, we'd take high school students up to Lake Shasta every summer for a week of houseboating, tubing, and wakeboarding. One year, a kid named Justin joined up. Justin was an absolute joy, upbeat, positive, and always game for something wild, whether on a tube or a wakeboard. Justin was also marginally Christian, and I remember heading into that week together, praying quietly in my mind that Jesus would draw him close and change his life.

About halfway through the week, I was driving a ski boat pulling Justin and another student on tubes. Per usual, Justin decided to jump from his tube to the other student's tube.

But he mistimed his leap and landed headfirst into the water, which at those speeds isn't a great feeling. We pulled Justin into the boat and could tell immediately that he was in bad shape. He said his neck was sore and he couldn't hear out of the ear that hit the water first. Concerned, I decided to drive him into town and get him checked out at the emergency room.

Long story short, we waited in the ER for hours. By the time a doctor was finally available, it was late into the evening and we hadn't eaten since breakfast. Thankfully, Justin wasn't hurt too seriously, and after getting the prescribed medicine, we drove to a nearby diner. Exhausted and famished, I told Justin to order whatever he wanted. I'd do the same. And we did. Burgers, fries, onion rings, milkshakes, and more. As the food came out, Justin asked to pray. I was surprised but thrilled. Maybe Jesus was answering the prayer, drawing him close. Justin began to pray for the food. Specifically. In great detail.

"God, thank you for these cheeseburgers. Thank you for the meat and the cheese and the bacon. Thank you for the people who made all of this. God, thanks for these fries and the ketchup we can dip them in."

On and on he went. I was starving. At a certain point, my stomach overwhelmed my heart and my mind and I grew annoyed. Until I opened my eyes and saw tears in Justin's eyes as he was expressing gratitude for the milkshakes, I think. Or was it the mozzarella sticks? I can't recall, and it doesn't matter. What I do remember is learning from this fifteen-year-old kid what it means to find gratitude and groundedness in daily bread.

After a heartfelt *amen*, we began to eat. After chatting for a few moments, Justin asked if we could read the Bible and discuss it while we ate. We spent several hours sitting in that booth reading and discussing long sections of the Gospel of John together. We walked into that diner famished. We left full. That's what daily bread does. It fills us up with strength for the day, and the day after that, and the day after that too.

Three

The God Who Sees in the "See-Me" World of Influencers

Pixelon was YouTube before YouTube. At least it wanted to be. In 1998 a man named Michael Fenne recruited a handful of skilled engineers to create a streaming video platform that would be accessible on anyone's internet browser. This was the late 1990s, when online video content was mostly grainy images endlessly loading through rackety dial-up modems. But the potential of high-quality streaming video on the internet was great. A potential financial windfall awaited.

As such, Fenne attracted a lot of attention. In December 1998, the company announced that Paramount Pictures would use its technology to promote its new Star Trek film, and Pixelon became a darling among venture capitalists with deep pockets looking to get in on what seemed to be a generational innovation ready to reinvent an entire industry. Within its first few months Pixelon had raised $35 million in early funding.

To celebrate his early success, Fenne threw a company launch party called iBash. Pixelon rented out the MGM

Grand in Las Vegas and booked Kiss, the Dixie Chicks, and
even convinced the Who to reunite for a private performance.
In total, the extravaganza cost the company $12 million. More
than one-third of all the money it'd raised in early funding
was blown on a single party. Court records have shown that
around the same time, a $22,000 invoice for the electrical
wiring system at the company's headquarters went unpaid.

There were plenty of problems at Pixelon, but two in particular stood out. First, its technology was a farce. It didn't
work. Fenne had promised to live stream the iBash launch
party from Las Vegas to Times Square in real time, but not a
single frame projected correctly. The second problem was an
even bigger one. Michael Fenne wasn't Michael Fenne. His
real name was David Kim Stanley, and he was on the state of
Virginia's most wanted list for stock fraud.

Pixelon, this revolutionary company, led by its brilliant,
innovative founder, was a sham. But no one would've believed
it during the Who's encore performance of "Won't Get Fooled
Again." For David Kim Stanley, the name of the game was
being seen.

Being seen as Michael Fenne.

Being seen as a genius entrepreneur.

Being seen as an industry-disrupting CEO.

But in reality, the last thing Stanley wanted was to be
truly seen.

Truly seen as a con man.

Truly seen as a fraud.

Truly seen as a criminal.

The desire to have all eyes on us can become all-consuming. And that desire has only grown exponentially in the decades since Pixelon, much of its increase fueled by the proliferation of influencers. Noting the near-religious fervor and allegiance many evoke, the writer Leigh Stein calls influencers "a different kind of clergy."[1] But ultimately this isn't about the influencers. It's about us. Stein continues, "The whole economy of Instagram is based on our thinking about our selves, posting about our selves, working on our selves." On my drive into the office every morning I pass by a local high school, and because there's a stoplight in front of the school, I usually sit awhile at a red light watching dozens of teenagers make their way slowly across the street toward first period. The lack of conversation and eye contact is astounding. Surrounded by each other, most of the students are locked in on screens. Not an uncommon scene. We stare at our screens, to see and be seen.

What's trending?

What do I need to know?

What is there to see?

How many likes?

How many comments?

How many shares?

Am I being seen?

THEATER AND TRUMPETS

I cut my teeth in local church ministry as a youth ministry intern. My first summer, we took about fifty high school students to Mexico on a mission trip, partnering with a local church to build houses for families living in impoverished neighborhoods. I was a twenty-two-year-old college kid overflowing with passion for ministry but completely devoid of any discernible skills relating to tools. Nevertheless, the youth pastor assigned me a group of students and told us we'd be responsible for constructing one of the walls of the house.

I was overwhelmed but did my best, meticulously studying the instruction manual and scrambling to get the job done and impress my boss. Hours into building, beaten down by the heat and my own stress, I sat to take a quick water break. Less than a minute or two into my well-deserved rest, the youth pastor, who hadn't walked over to our area all day, made his way toward us. During my break, another intern, a dear friend, had stepped in to lead the students while I hydrated. My boss saw our progress, looked right at the other intern, and said, "Great job, man."

"Great job, man?" Which man? Oh, that man, the one that's been at it for all of 120 seconds? This was criminal! I'd been robbed of my well-deserved, hard-earned recognition. I was seething.

In the middle of his famed Sermon on the Mount, Jesus teaches us to "Be careful not to practice your righteousness in front of others to be seen by them" (Matthew 6:1). When it comes to the world of social media influencers, there isn't a whole lot we'd call righteous, per se, but practicing righteousness in the first-century Jewish world was a specific and, for some, somewhat technical exercise. In the subsequent verses, Jesus addresses three specific practices of righteousness:

Giving to the needy (Matthew 6:2)
Praying (Matthew 6:5)
Fasting (Matthew 6:16)

At the time, the local synagogue was the center of religious and societal life in every Jewish community, and every synagogue directed its people toward these three specific practices as practices of righteousness, practical ways of embodying and living in right relationship with God and one another. But when the practices become the point, right relationship can devolve into ritual keeping, and before long, practices intended to draw us closer to God become meaningless.

Again, Jesus' words in Matthew 6:1: "Be careful not to practice your righteousness in front of others *to be seen* by them" (emphasis added).

The phrase "to be seen" is the translation of a single Greek word, *theathenai*, from which we get the English word *theater*. Jesus is warning against practicing righteousness as theater, a performance intended to elicit accolades and applause.

Jesus continues, "So when you give to the needy, do not

announce it with *trumpets*, as the hypocrites do in the synagogues and on the streets, to be honored by others. Truly I tell
you, they have received their reward in full. But when you give
to the needy, do not let your left hand know what your right
hand is doing, so that your giving may be in secret" (Matthew
6:2–4, emphasis added).

In Jesus' day, giving to the needy was an organized effort in
each Jewish community. People would give financially to the
synagogue, and the synagogue would then take the funds and
provide collectively for those in need within the community.
In most synagogues, people would drop their coins into boxes
made of a ram's horn, which was also used to craft traditional
Jewish trumpets called shofars.

This is a brilliant play on words. Jesus is essentially saying, "When you drop your coins for the poor into the giving
box, don't do it loudly, don't do it performatively, don't blow
the trumpet so everyone hears your generosity." He continues
by saying that this is what the "hypocrites" do. The word in
Greek was originally used to describe theater actors.

Theater and trumpets. This is what the actors on social
media do. They're playing parts, lulling us into the suspension
of belief, and seeking our admiration, adulation, and applause.
But it's all for show.

Don't live this way, Jesus says.

But this is a preposterous proposal in the be-seen-or-
don't-matter world of influencers. What are they without likes,
comments, shares, retweets, and an ever-expanding cadre

of followers? Increasing their following is impossible without playing the part. Without theater, the whole structure collapses.

One influencer admits, "It only helps to have a following. I'm not offended when people call me an influencer rather than an actress, because it's all the same," while another puts it simply, "We are all actors."[2] Being seen is big business, and almost all of what's presented to us by influencers is essentially a sales pitch disguised as real life.

A few years ago, a lifestyle influencer named Sydney Pugh went to a popular coffee shop in LA called Alfred's. After purchasing a drink with her own money, she posted about it as if she'd struck a sponsorship deal.[3] Another influencer took a personal vacation to Miami, paying her own way, but took the time to post throughout, carefully captioning photos so as to imply sponsorships with the restaurants and venues she was visiting. She admitted, "You say it in a way that people could interpret it as you having an established relationship with that brand... The hope is that it's perceived in a way that looks like there's a reason you're in a different city and state, not just enjoying a weekend vacation."[4] Even when influencers aren't paid to sell, they're selling.

A fifteen-year-old influencer named Allie puts it plainly: "People pretend to have brand deals to seem cool. It's like, 'I got this for free while all you losers are paying.'"[5] Most are aware of the con, but we keep playing along anyway. The journalist Taylor Lorenz notes that "A decade ago, shilling products to your fans may have been seen as selling out. Now it's a sign of success."[6] Granted, most of us aren't social media influencers, so we might think it safe to assume we aren't doing much shilling. But many if not most of us are living in the wake of the be-seen culture of influencers, and we're drowning.

Researchers Jonathan Haidt and Jean Twenge are two of the leading voices in the conversation around the impact of smartphones and social media on Americans in general and teenagers in particular. Beginning in 2012, they noticed a significant and sharp increase in teen depression, loneliness, suicide, and self-harm, and they were puzzled. There hadn't been any significant cultural or national crisis that might've triggered such a widespread and considerable change. Nothing, that is, except social media. They "discovered that 2012 was the first year that a majority of Americans owned a smartphone; by 2015, two-thirds of teens did too. This was also the period when social media use moved from optional to ubiquitous among adolescents."[7] They also noted that the "compare and despair" culture perpetuated by these platforms had created a catastrophic intersection, inhabited by the online masses, between the inexorable longing to be seen and the unrelenting sense of being totally unseen. This is an untenable juxtaposition.

Increase is the name of the be-seen world of influencers. Increase reach, followers, sponsorships, brand, and influence, even if it means faking your way to the top. And all the while, we play along, suspending belief and thrusting ourselves into the destructive vortex of the comparison game, fooling ourselves into believing that being seen is the path to meaning, purpose, and significance.

But this constant and laborious leaning up-and-to-the-right never actually leads to anything substantive; it never leads to the full sort of life Jesus offers us. Instead, the ongoing chase for more leaves us simply more exhausted and depleted, at the end of ourselves and ultimately alone and unseen.

What we need is a different way, a paradoxical and subversive path downward, away from the relentless pursuit of fifteen minutes of fame and toward the beautiful and quiet calm of anonymity. What we need is the good news of *less*, a gospel of *decrease*.

I MUST DECREASE

John the Baptist was a big deal. As he preached and baptized in the wilderness, the masses were drawn to him, coming from near and far, "from Jerusalem and all Judea and the whole region of the Jordan. Confessing their sins, they were baptized by him in the Jordan River" (Matthew 3:5–6). John was in some ways a first-century influencer. But as the prominence of his cousin Jesus began to rise, John's followers grew concerned and sought a strategy to guard their hero's cultural influence.

They came to John and said to him, "Rabbi, the one who

was with you across the Jordan, to whom you testified, here he is baptizing, and all are going to him" (John 3:26 NRSV).

Today in parts of Iraq and Iran, there is a religious group known as the Mandaeans, who revere John the Baptist as the great prophet of their religion. Baptism is not a singular sacramental moment in a Mandaean believer's life, as it is in Christian tradition. Rather, influenced by the stories of John the Baptist baptizing in the Jordan River, the Mandaeans are baptized and rebaptized weekly. Mandaean baptisms always take place in rivers deemed worthy, which are called *yardenas*, after the River Jordan.

Through their piety and devotion, the Mandaeans reflect their hero. Week after week, over and over, they get baptized, but they fail to recognize that baptism is a singular moment: God gives us new life, once and for all, upon being raised from the water. To be baptized over and over, without finding life, is to work in vain. The Mandaeans have taken the practices modeled by John the Baptist and have made them the point. But the practices are never the point. Likewise, mirroring influencers as we do is done in vain. We do it over and over, but never find life.

The twentieth-century Belgian painter René Magritte was famous for his surrealist art, which pushed against the limits of the canvas and confronted the viewer's sense of reality. Two of his most well-known pieces are a pair, *The Human Condition*, painted in 1933, and *The Human Condition II*, painted in 1935.

Both are paintings within paintings, depicting easels inside rooms, in front of windows to the outside world. The paintings on the easels are without frames and depict a contiguous, almost imperceptible transition from themselves to the realities they seek to display. Upon first viewing, our minds immediately assume that the paintings within the paintings depict whatever part of the landscape is hidden from view by the canvases. But Magritte's point was to critique this assumption and remind us that the entire thing is a single painted image. There is no landscape behind the canvas. There is only the actual canvas and the very real lines, colors, and contours painted upon it by Magritte himself. And even still, it is difficult to look at these paintings without yearning to believe there is something hidden from view.

This might be why Magritte called both pieces *The Human Condition*. We so often choose to trust the mirage and are even eager to suspend actual belief to do so. The canvas of the smartphone screen is no exception. We know influencers are shilling products and that their curated images of the good life aren't real life. But we're compelled by the illusion anyway. We yearn for what we know isn't there. We go about our real lives longing for the life that isn't.

As the pressure to measure up mounts, we grow weary, but relentless pressure of comparison keeps us climbing. Yet the mountains of comparison have no peaks. They elevate endlessly. And most insidiously, they are not mountains at all but long roads down into deep valleys. We are journeying upside down, believing the path is leading us upward when in fact it is leading us into the depths of despair and isolation.

This is why the upside-down nature of God's kingdom is in fact right side up, if only we'd have the eyes to see. Back to John the Baptist and his concerned followers. They were alarmed that "all are going to [Jesus]" (John 3:26 NRSV), inferring that John was facing the grave threat of losing followers, which meant losing influence. If being seen was the greatest value, this was a death blow. But John saw things properly. What seemed upside down to others he knew to be right side up. "He must increase, but I must decrease" (John 3:30 NRSV).

Decrease was the way up. Henri Nouwen once wrote that "The way of the Christian leader is not the way of upward mobility in which our world has invested so much, but the way of downward mobility ending on the cross."[8] This isn't true just for leaders but for all of us. And in fact, the willingness to decrease so that Christ might increase is the marker of true Christian leadership. This is Nouwen's point.

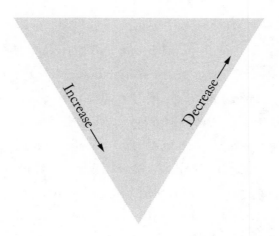

It's certainly easier to be seen standing atop the mountain. But the footing up there (or down there, in the upside-down kingdom) is narrow and unsure. It's far from steady ground. Planting our feet firmly on low ground, on the humble, unmoving, sure foundation of dirt and soil and earth, is where we find enough stability not only for ourselves but to hold others up as well. And this is where we are truly seen. The attention of the masses aspiring to do what you do is but a fleeting glance. A deep and abiding gaze from the one who doesn't look away is always reserved for those who offer sacrificial love and humble service.

This is why Jesus, regardless of what a person does or does not believe about his divinity, continues to be the most significant figure in human history. Because he embodied the powerful right side up of upside down, as the apostle Paul explains:

> In your relationships with one another, have the same mindset as Christ Jesus: Who, being in very nature God, did not consider equality with God something to be used to his own advantage; rather, he made himself nothing by taking the very nature of a servant, being made in human likeness. And being found in appearance as a man, he humbled himself by becoming obedient to death—even death on a cross! Therefore God exalted him to the highest place and gave him the name that is above every name, that at the name of Jesus every knee should bow, in heaven and on earth and under the earth, and every tongue acknowledge that Jesus Christ is Lord, to the glory of God the Father. (Philippians 2:5–11)

The Nike swoosh. The McDonald's M. Iconic brands to be sure. Recognizable immediately, globally. But they do not compare to the symbol of the cross. The cross is without question the most universally recognized brand in history. In our world, does it get any more upside down than that? A Roman instrument of death reserved in the first-century world for criminals deemed most deserving of a humiliating execution is now the most recognizable symbol of power, strength, and authority. Jesus goes down to the grave via the cross, and today it is the most seen brand on the planet.

The way down is the way to be seen.

The way to be seen is to see those who are unseen.

Laying oneself down is the way to lift oneself up.

Service and sacrifice are the markers of true influence.

I must decrease. He must increase.

THE GOD WHO SEES

Let's go back for a moment to Jesus' teaching in Matthew 6. Just before teaching his disciples to pray what we now commonly call the Lord's Prayer, Jesus instructs them this way:

> And when you pray, do not be like the hypocrites, for they love to pray standing in the synagogues and on the street corners to be seen by others. Truly I tell you, they have received their reward in full. But when you pray, go into your room, close the door and pray to your Father, who is unseen. (Matthew 6:5–6)

The phrase "to be seen" here is the Greek word *phaino*, which is most often translated into English as "to shine." Think spotlight. The longing to be seen is a longing for the spotlight. Jesus is essentially saying, "Don't seek the spotlight."

At my best, the reason I do some of the work that I do—writing, speaking, serving in the local church—is because I am deeply compelled by the life, teachings, death, resurrection, and ascension of Jesus and because my great desire is to tell as many people as I can as convincingly as I can about him. But at my worst, I have ulterior motives.

I was born in South Korea and moved to the United States as a toddler. The only child of an immigrant mother working multiple jobs to make ends meet, I spent those early years at home with my aunt, who spoke only Korean. Then, all of a sudden, at age six, I was plopped into first grade. I didn't speak a lick of English, and I certainly couldn't read or write it. I was ostracized, an alien navigating the foreign soil of public school.

This was almost four decades ago, but the pain of that season still lingers somewhere deep in my body. I carry it with me. So at my worst, I do the work I do to prove a point.

Sure, the kids made fun of me because I couldn't communicate.

But look at me now. People pay me to talk.

Sure, I couldn't read and write back then.

But look at me now. People pay me to read and write.

At my worst, in my most shamed and unseen state, I do what I do because I long for the spotlight. I long to be seen.

And most of the time, I live in the tension between my best and worst self. By God's grace and with plenty of counseling, I've begun to experience significant healing from old wounds in recent years. But I've still got a long way to go. My guess is that you do too. And that's okay. We're okay. God sees us. He always has and always will.

In Luke 8, we read the story of a woman who suffered from a debilitating and humiliating condition, "subject to bleeding for twelve years" (v. 43). In the Jewish world at the time, her infirmity made her socially and ceremonially "unclean," in the religious language of the day. This meant that for twelve years she'd lived as an outcast, cut off from her family, friends, and society as a whole. She was a forgotten woman, wholly and utterly unseen.

When this woman heard that Jesus of Nazareth was coming through her town, she seized the opportunity and "came up behind him and touched the edge of his cloak" (Luke 8:44). To do such a thing was to literally risk life and limb. Unclean individuals were legally prohibited from having any physical contact with anyone, much less a Jewish rabbi. So why does she do this?

At the time, most Jewish men and certainly all Jewish rabbis, including Jesus, regularly wore traditional prayer shawls over their outer clothing. When they prayed, they'd lift the shawl over their heads, creating a wing-like shape with the edges. Because of this, the edges of the prayer shawl were called *kanaph*, which is the Hebrew word for "wings."

There was also at the time a popular messianic prophecy from the book of Malachi: "But for you who fear my name, the sun of righteousness shall rise with healing in its *wings*" (Malachi 4:2 ESV, emphasis added). Because of this prophetic verse, many believed that when the Messiah arrived, there would be literal healing in the wings, the edges, of his prayer shawl.

This unseen woman sees Jesus, believes he is the Messiah with healing in his wings, and sneaks through the crowd, hoping to remain unseen, in hopes of finding healing. Then, "immediately her bleeding stopped" (Luke 8:44).

The risk ends up being worth the reward, and then some. The unseen woman is healed, all is well, and she's on her way. Until she's not.

> "Who touched me?" Jesus asked. When they all denied it, Peter said, "Master, the people are crowding and pressing against you." But Jesus said, "Someone touched me; I know that power has gone out from me." Then the woman, seeing that she could not go unnoticed, came trembling and fell at his feet. In the presence of all the people, she told why she had touched him and how she had been instantly healed. Then he said to her, "Daughter, your faith has healed you. Go in peace." (Luke 8:45–48)

Jesus doesn't just heal the unclean woman.

Jesus sees the unseen woman. He calls her daughter.

Maybe you feel unseen. Or unclean. Ostracized and marginalized. Forgotten and unwanted.

In a culture that platforms and parades being seen as a high virtue, obscurity feels like death.

But Jesus sees you.

One final return to Matthew 6. Woven throughout Jesus' admonition to seek anonymity is a reminder that the gospel of decreasing oneself does not mean becoming invisible. Quite the opposite. Jesus says in our quiet faithfulness, away from the accolades and applause so many are desperate for, we are truly seen. Three separate times—in verses 4, 6, and 18—Jesus repeats the same hopeful refrain: "Your Father, who *sees* what is done in secret, will reward you."

The word for "secret" is the Greek word *kryptos*, which essentially means "hidden." God sees us in the quiet obscurity of our lives. And if God sees us, we are truly seen, in ways no amount of spotlight or influence could ever offer.

This is the gift God gives us—his deep, abiding gaze.

This is the same gift the church can offer the world.

THE CHURCH THAT SEES

A couple of winters ago, I saw a young woman sitting in her car in our church parking lot. It was a Sunday, about an hour before our first service. I asked her if she needed help. She told me her name was Margaret and that she was waiting to meet with one of our pastors. I let her into the front office so she could wait in the warmth. Her eyes carried a deep loneliness and her shoulders slumped, weighed down by a heavy sadness that was almost palpable. A few moments later, our care pastor walked in and they began talking. I stepped into my office and prayed for Margaret. Thinking back to that moment, I realize now that Margaret showed up that morning on the off chance that the church might be the one place where she might be seen, a last-ditch effort to redeem a life lived in painful obscurity. Let me explain.

Toward the end of his letter to the early Christians in Colossae, the apostle Paul writes a series of greetings to friends and includes this note: "Tychicus will tell you all the news about me. He is a dear brother, a faithful minister and fellow servant in the Lord. I am sending him to you for the express purpose that you may know about our circumstances and that he may encourage your hearts" (Colossians 4:7–8).

Paul calls his friend Tychicus a "fellow servant." In Greek, the two words are one: *syndoulas*, which means "co-slave." Paul calls Tychicus a co-slave, indicating that he himself is also a slave, along with Tychicus. This matters for a number of reasons, but specifically because of the person he mentions next: "He is coming with Onesimus, our faithful and dear brother, who is one of you" (Colossians 4:9).

There's another book in the New Testament called Philemon, which is the name of the person to whom the book is addressed. It's a personal letter from Paul. Philemon was a wealthy Christian in Colossae, very likely one of the financial benefactors of the church there and a respected leader among the Colossian Christians. The church gathered in his home, and tradition tells us that he was eventually martyred for his faith under the rule of the Roman emperor Nero.

As a wealthy man in the Greco-Roman world, Philemon had slaves. It's important to note that slavery in the ancient world was quite different from what most of us think of when we think of slavery. Today, *slavery* most often refers to the transatlantic slave trade, when Europeans brutally kidnapped men and women from Africa, against their will, to sell them as property. This type of slavery, while it did exist, was not the predominant form of slavery in the ancient world.

This is not to say that slavery in any form was or is a part of God's plan for human flourishing. Far from it. And we see this most clearly in Paul's teaching here.

The word for "slave" is the Greek word *doulas*, and it's better translated as "servant" or "bondservant." In the ancient world, it was common practice for people to sell themselves as servants to wealthy households, typically to pay a debt or escape poverty. Scholars estimate that up to 20 percent of the Greco-Roman population were slaves, or servants, during the time when much of the New Testament was being written.[9]

In his letter to the Galatian Christians, Paul writes this: "So in Christ Jesus you are all children of God through faith, for all of you who were baptized into Christ have clothed yourselves with Christ. There is neither Jew nor Gentile, *neither slave nor free*, nor is there male and female, for you are all one in Christ Jesus" (Galatians 3:26–28, emphasis added).

"Neither slave nor free." We are all one.

The story of the Bible is in many ways the story of the

unseen being seen. Those wrongly deemed property by society are embraced as people—and even more than that, as sons and daughters—by the God in whose image we are all made.

This is why Paul's concluding remarks to the Colossian Christians are so powerful. Remember, he refers to Tychicus and himself as co-slaves, while he calls Onesimus a "faithful and dear brother, who is one of you."

Paul's letter to Philemon reveals that Onesimus was once a slave in Philemon's house. But he runs away. Reading between the lines, most scholars believe that Onesimus fled not because he was mistreated but because he'd done something wrong; it's very likely that Onesimus stole from Philemon. While on the run, Onesimus runs into Paul, encounters Christ in a transformative way, and becomes a follower of Jesus. And now Paul is sending Onesimus back to Colossae, which means he's sending him back to Philemon.

Onesimus, once a slave, wrongs his "master" and makes a run for it. On the run, his only comfort might have been his familiarity with obscurity. He'd spent most of his life unseen. And now, being unseen was critical to his safety.

But Onesimus ends up being seen.

By Paul. By Christ.

And now, he must return to the man he wronged. Paul advocates for him and implores Philemon to see Onesimus the way he does, the way Christ does. Presumably, some people in Colossae would've known about Onesimus's wrongdoing. They would've known he was a slave who stole and ran. And here's Paul, one of the key leaders of the Christian movement, calling himself a slave and calling Onesimus "a faithful and dear brother, who is one of you."

Paul is leveling the playing field. In fact, in his letter to Philemon, Paul makes the point even more abundantly clear. He writes:

> Perhaps the reason he was separated from you for a little while was that you might have him back forever— no longer as a slave, but better than a slave, as a dear brother. He is very dear to me but even dearer to you, both as a fellow man and as a brother in the Lord. So if you consider me a partner, welcome him as you would welcome me. (Philemon 15–17)

Paul is saying, "Philemon, you have Onesimus back, but not for a contracted set of years; you have him back forever. And not forever as a slave or servant. He is your brother now. Welcome him as you would welcome me. See him for who he truly is."

This is what happens in the kingdom of God.

Slaves and masters become brothers and sisters.

Enemies become friends, and friends become family.

In the see-and-be-seen world of influencers, inundated with much to see but no one actually seeing or being seen, the church can and must become a truly *seeing* community.

The church that *sees* is the church that invites, welcomes, and holds the stories of those in our midst with care, compassion, and empathy.

The church that *sees* is the church that strives to stand together. Though the color of our skin may differ, our politics may differ, our opinions may differ, and our perspectives, stories, hopes, dreams, anxieties, and fears may differ, the church that *sees* stands alongside one another in love, for we are all one in Jesus Christ our King.

The Sunday that I met Margaret, we were celebrating baptisms in our services. A few minutes before our last service of the day, the pastor who'd met with Margaret earlier in the morning told me that she wanted to get baptized.

I then learned that not long before I met her, Margaret had been standing on the edge of a bridge in the darkness of early morning. She was moments away from jumping off, taking a few deep breaths to ready herself for a swift descent into death. She thought no one would notice or care. She thought no one would see. Why would she think otherwise? No one had seen her thus far in her life.

But at that exact moment, a woman happened to be driving over that bridge. She pulled over, got out of her car, and asked Margaret to please step down from the edge. She saw Margaret. After some conversation, Margaret stepped away from the precipice and toward a person who genuinely cared for her, maybe for the first time. Long story short, she was told of our church and put in contact with our pastor, and shortly after, I was opening the door of our office to her.

A couple of hours after that, Margaret stood with that pastor in the waters of life, seen and loved by God, seen and loved by hundreds of men and women cheering her on into the kingdom.

Margaret descended into death that morning.

Death of obscurity and ostracization.

Death of isolation and loneliness.

Death of desperation and despair.

And she rose from the waters.

She rose anew—seen, known, and loved by the God who sees.

The God who sees us all.

Four

Screaming to Belong

A close friend texted me one morning in a panic. A day earlier he'd posted on his social media accounts what he thought was a fairly benign opinion about some political matter. I know what you're thinking. No political matter is "fairly benign" these days. Nevertheless, the virality of his post was unexpected and unwanted, and it came as a shock. There were a handful of affirmations, but mostly, the online masses came out of the woodwork to scrutinize, criticize, nitpick, and split hairs. They came with their torches to set fire to his credibility. They came to cancel my friend.

Most were distant online acquaintances. Some were trolls looking for another nameless, faceless victim to devour. But many of the incensed were friends he'd known personally, some for many years. At one point, he texted me, "Outrage culture is decimating my real life friendships." Decimate is right.

For centuries, Rome was a global superpower. At the height of its dominance, the empire ruled from modern-day

England to India. The backbone of Roman ascendence was its military, which relied heavily on ruthless discipline. Roman soldiers were heavily armored at the chest, but their backs were uncovered in battle, the thought being that there was never an instance when it'd be appropriate to turn and retreat. Any soldiers who failed to hold their position were publicly punished. One-tenth of the group would be chosen at random and bludgeoned to death. In Latin, the word for "ten" is *decem*. This is where we get the word *decimate*, which today has taken on the meaning "destroy."

A random selection eliminated.

Impulsive cancellation.

Such brutality contributed to Rome's rise for a time. But eventually, Rome burned. A culture built on decimation was decimated.

OUTRAGE AND TRIBALISM

Widespread outrage is not a new phenomenon, but the rise of social media has pressurized us all in a unique way. Much like in Rome, there is in our culture today an increasingly incessant and insatiable hunger for elimination. Cancel culture has a quota. Someone, or more accurately many some-ones, must go. And the bar for revocation is ever changing. What matters most is that there be a target for the outrage. As Jonathan Haidt puts it, "Social media has both magnified and weaponized the frivolous."[1] The bow is perpetually drawn and the arrows must fly, justified or not.

The digital age perpetuates this because outrage sells. Angry and vociferous posts garner the most engagement online. Studies have shown that "outrageous content generates more revenue through viral sharing, natural selection-like forces may favour 'supernormal' stimuli that trigger much stronger outrage responses than do transgressions we typically encounter in everyday life."[2] The internet amplifies outrage, increasing its volume and velocity in ways typically unseen in person. It's easier to scream at an avatar on a screen than a real human face-to-face.

Simultaneously, outrage is proving grossly ineffective when it comes to actual change. It has little to no effect on real opinions or real-life circumstances on the ground. It's more about what the writer Ashley Charles calls "clicktivism," which she describes as "the modern-day picket sign for the work-shy yet well intentioned who share their outrage through hashtags, online petitions and rambling captions about equal rights."[3] She continues, "Had a long day and couldn't get round to any real protesting? You need clicktivism! Feel like supporting a political campaign but also feel like taking an afternoon nap?...I know just the thing...clicktivism!" Because of its ease and accessibility, clicktivism has set our online lives ablaze with rage, leading people like neuroscientist Molly Crockett to ask, "If moral outrage is a fire, is the internet like gasoline?"[4] The answer is yes. As Rome once did, we are burning today in an inferno of our own making.

Our militant at-the-ready posture toward one another has led to a deep and hostile division pervading our nation, cities and towns, neighborhoods and schools, workplaces and social circles, friendships, families, homes, and churches. We've become enslaved to tribalism. The political analyst Martin Gurri assesses our current condition this way:

> [There used to be] massive numbers of people all essentially looking into a gigantic mirror in which they saw themselves reflected. So most people were consuming the same content and there was a common denominator. The digital revolution has shattered that mirror, and now the public inhabits those broken pieces of glass. So the public isn't one thing; it's highly fragmented, and it's basically mutually hostile. It's mostly people yelling at each other and living in bubbles of one sort or another.[5]

In an age of outrage and tribalism, it isn't eggshells we're walking on. It's shattered glass. The damage done is far more severe as we bleed our humanity all over the cold concrete of division and polarization. The irony, though, is that outrage and tribalism themselves are fragile outer shells, protective coverings tenuously harboring delicate human souls longing for more.

The writer Parker Palmer describes the soul as a wild animal. He writes, "If we want to see a wild animal, we know that the last thing we should do is go crashing through the woods yelling for it to come out. But if we will walk quietly into the woods, sit patiently at the base of a tree, breathe with the earth, and fade into our surroundings, the wild creature we seek might put in an appearance."[6] Outrage is like crashing through the woods. In response, our souls take flight toward the covering of either isolation or the faux safety of tribes tenuously and temporarily held together by a thinly shared opinion.

The truth is, almost no one *wants* to be outraged and tribalistic. Most people desire healthy relationships and societies built on meaningful connections. Most people want to *belong*. But because of all the anger and division, we've come to believe that real belonging is impossible, leaving us perplexed, frustrated, and alone. We are exhausted. But we are in fact more connected by our exhaustion than we might know.

According to a comprehensive research report called Hidden Tribes, when it comes to politics—no doubt the source of our rage—67 percent of Americans categorically belong to what they call the "exhausted majority."[7] These are ideologically flexible individuals who support working toward compromise but who feel fatigued and forgotten in the political landscape. If that sounds a bit like you, then you're like most people today.

You'd never know it from social media and the twenty-four-hour news cycle, but most of us aren't as outraged and tribalistic as you've been led to believe. Most are simply and thoroughly exhausted. Most are lonely, isolated, and searching for belonging, like you and like me.

SCREAMING TO BELONG

In February 2021, Harvard University conducted a vast research study to measure loneliness in our country and found that:

- 36 percent of all Americans identify as being "lonely all or almost all the time."[8]
- 61 percent of those between 18–25 say they're "lonely all or almost all the time."[9]
- 63 percent of young adults suffer high rates of loneliness, anxiety, and depression.[10]
- 42 percent of those between 18–34 say they "always feel left out."[11]

Take a look at this graph.[12]

It measures loneliness at school among teenagers—"at school" is the operative phrase. This isn't loneliness while alone. This is loneliness while surrounded by dozens of classmates

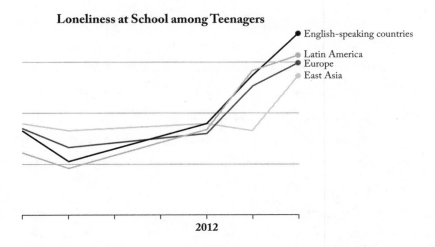

Loneliness at School among Teenagers

English-speaking countries

Latin America
Europe
East Asia

2012

and hundreds, maybe thousands, of fellow teenagers through-out the school day.

Notice that there is a very clear spike upward about two-thirds of the way across the horizontal axis, a timeline ranging from the early 2000s to the late 2010s. The significant spike upward in loneliness occurs right around 2012, which was the year that smartphones became ubiquitous in the hands of teenagers. It was also the year Facebook bought Instagram. At the end of 2011, Instagram had about 15 million active users. By the end of 2012, that number was 100 million. Today, Instagram has more than 2 billion active users.[13]

The correlation here of loneliness with smartphone and social media use is not coincidental nor insignificant. The pervasiveness of the smartphone and the all-consuming, magnetic allure of social media are spiraling an entire generation into a vortex of isolation, depression, and despair.[14]

Though we are living in an increasingly digitally interconnected world, we are personally disconnected, which has led us to a crisis of *belonging*. In her aptly titled book *Alone Together*, MIT professor Sherry Turkle writes: "We are lonely but fearful of intimacy. Digital connections...may offer the illusion of companionship without the demands of friendship. Our networked life allows us to hide from each other, even as we are tethered to each other. We'd rather text than talk."[15]

Many of us, I'm sure, are familiar with Abraham Maslow's hierarchy of needs, developed by the psychologist in 1943. To put it simply, the hierarchy of needs is a way of mapping how human beings prioritize their motivations and behaviors.

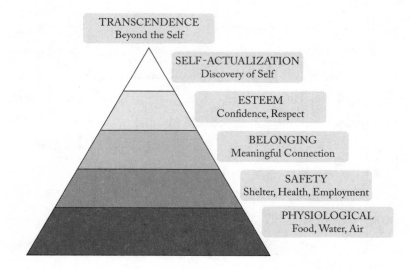

At the base of the pyramid is the most fundamental motivating factor for human behavior, physiological need—food, water, breathable air, and so on. Imagine a leisurely boat ride with a friend. The water is calm, the sun warms your back, and the two of you are having a deep conversation about life and the search for meaning. All is well until your friend stands up to stretch, loses his balance, and falls into the water. Imagine also that this friend is not wearing a life jacket and does not know how to swim. Panic ensues, for him at least. Now, imagine the unthinkable—that you simply continue chatting on, asking him about his aspirational desires, not noticing his desperate need for immediate help.

What would be happening to your friend in this case? At this point, he'd care less about conversing deeply about the meaning of life—indeed, in the grand scheme of things, an essential conversation—and care only about saving his actual life. This is Maslow's hierarchy of needs. Only when our more primal needs are met can we rise up toward the more complex, nuanced, and meaningful needs of human experience. But as you move up the pyramid, assuming that your baseline needs are met, other human needs, motivating factors, and behaviors begin to arise.

So once physiological needs—food, water, and so on—are met, there are safety needs—shelter, health, employment, and so on. From there, the pyramid moves upward toward belonging—the human need for meaningful connection and relationships. Then there's what Maslow calls esteem, which is self-confidence and respect from others. Above that is self-actualization, which is essentially about discovering and developing self-identity and, from that, finding a hope for life. Finally, in his later years, Maslow added a final category at the very top of the pyramid called transcendence, which is the search for meaning beyond the self.

For all intents and purposes, the hierarchy of needs is a secular tool, but it identifies fundamentally human, and therefore spiritual, needs. When Maslow talks about transcendence, for followers of Jesus, we would view that as the search for God. And for self-actualization, we'd understand that as the search for identity, which we ultimately find in Christ.

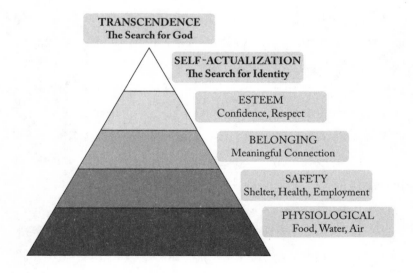

Chances are you're reading this book, a Christian book, because somewhere along the way you found your identity and hope in Christ. You discovered that the search for God was not in vain, that God can indeed be found, or better yet, that you could be found by God. But think for a moment about your very early days with God, the infancy of your faith in Christ, when your heart and mind first encountered the truth of the Gospel. Who's there?

You, of course. And Jesus, yes. Solid Christian answer.

But who else?

Maybe a parent or a grandparent.

Maybe a small-group leader.

A youth pastor.

A friend who invited you to church.

Maybe a youth group. Or a campus ministry.

Very likely a local church community.

The point is that for many, if not most—if not all of us—at some point we were found by God and discovered our identity in Christ, we encountered the truth of the gospel, and this cataclysmic, transformative reorienting of our lives unfolded within, through, and into the loving care of a community of *belonging*.

On our journey toward identity and toward God himself, we found Christ-centered communities anchored in truth that didn't shun us but rather welcomed us with open arms, with all of our doubts and confusion and brokenness and shame, in spite of our differences and divisions. And this community lovingly walked alongside us, as slowly as necessary, never wavering off the true path but always trekking along at a communal pace, a pace we could keep up with.

Outrage and tribalism threaten this all-important journey. They amplify our differences and divisions, feed off them, and divert us from both discovering our truest identity in Christ and God himself. Instead we are led down paths of cheap carbon copies of "belonging."

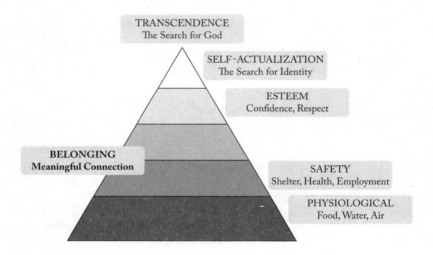

All the while, there's a dangerous deception at play. As we shout from our tribe toward opposing tribes, we are galvanized in our tribe and come to believe that this is what belonging looks like. This is one of the reasons why so many cultural movements today can build momentum so quickly. The opportunity to take part in the collective energy of a group bound together is like a stream in the desert of isolation. To the parched soul of the lonely, it doesn't matter where the stream came from or where it's headed; all we know is it's water and we're thirsty and sooner than we can think, we drink.

This is the challenge and opportunity before us. Followers of Jesus are called to do the difficult and beautiful work of carving paths of belonging through all the outrage and tribalism, paths paved by grace and truth, and made accessible to the lonely, isolated, and all those in despair. Together, as Christians, we must declare loudly and clearly, boldly and beautifully, that *belonging* is possible—deep, meaningful belonging, to God and his people.

The apostle Paul reminded the first Christians in Ephesus, "You are no longer foreigners and strangers, but fellow citizens with God's people and also members of his household, built on the foundation of the apostles and prophets, with Christ Jesus himself as the chief cornerstone" (Ephesians 2:19–20).

No longer foreigners and strangers but citizens and members of his household. The phrase *members of his household* was shorthand for extended family in the ancient world and in the original text is conveyed by the single Greek word *oikeioi*. The Greek word for "strangers" is *paroikoi*. Both words share the same root word—*oikos*—meaning "home."

"Strangers," or *paroikoi*, are those who dwell near or next to a home.

"Members of a household," or *oikeioi*, are those who dwell within a home.

Strangers and family are closer than we think. Eugene

Peterson beautifully paraphrases Ephesians 2:19–20 this way: "This kingdom of faith is now your home country. You're no longer strangers or outsiders. You *belong* here, with as much right to the name Christian as anyone. God is building a home. He's using us all—irrespective of how we got here—in what he is building" (MSG).

You belong here. This is the path people are desperate for. In her book *The Gospel Comes with a House Key*, Rosaria Butterfield reminds us that "this transition from stranger to neighbor to family does not happen naturally but only with intent and grit and sacrifice and God's blessing."[16]

Intent. Grit. Sacrifice. It won't be easy, and it will be costly. Specifically, combating outrage and tribalism and inviting people to belong will demand the intent, grit, and sacrifice necessary to see clearly in an age when so many are seeing red.

That etymology of the euphemism *seeing red* is thought to come from a couple of sources, both violent and hostile. It's possible that the phrase is connected to the idea of using red flags among ancient militaries to signal preparations for battle. Others believe the phrase comes from the sport of bullfighting and the signature red muleta used by matadors to incite raging bulls. Ironically, bulls are blind to the color red. It is in fact the matador's movement of the muleta that enrages the beast.

And so it is with outrage and tribalism. We see red and

we charge. But in reality, we're colorblind. We're not seeing what we think we're seeing. In order to empathetically and compassionately hear and respond to the longing for belonging beneath the anger, we must first learn to see clearly.

PLANK IN THE EYE

I was a lonely kid most of my life. My mother struggled to make ends meet for much of my childhood, which meant moving from apartment to apartment, looking for new job opportunities and cheaper rent. I went to four elementary schools in five years, making it nearly impossible to establish meaningful friendships.

I wrote earlier in the book about my inability to speak English when I entered first grade, and so on my first day of school I was immediately placed in an English as a second language class. I was the only kid in the class and spent most of that year completely ostracized from my fellow students.

One of the earliest memories I have from that year is from a day when my mom had packed me *kimbap*, which is essentially Korean sushi. This was before sushi was mainstream. When the other kids eating their PB&Js, sloppy joes, and rectangular pizzas saw my seaweed-wrapped rice, there was immediate uproar.

"Gross!"

"What are you eating?"

"That's not food!"

I'd gone from being unseen to having all eyes on me for the worst reasons. One moment, I'd wanted nothing more than to be noticed; the next moment, I was willing to give anything to disappear. I loathed being invisible, and yet, in that very moment, I wanted to be nothing but invisible.

This is my earliest memory of feeling judged. I was six, but I recall the emotions vividly—feelings of being judged sear themselves into our hearts because it makes us feel simultaneously exposed and yet unseen.

When we judge, we don't see clearly. We see red.

And in turn, tragically, the one being judged begins to see the same. Anger ensues, and, looking for cover, we divide into our groups, and the cycle of judgment continues.

In his book *Talking to Strangers*, Malcolm Gladwell writes, "We think we can easily see into the hearts of others based on the flimsiest of clues. We jump at the chance to judge strangers. We would never do that to ourselves, of course. We are nuanced and complex and enigmatic. But the stranger is easy."[17] We rarely afford others the generous benefit of the doubt we afford ourselves.

This is heartbreaking, not just for the one being judged but for the one judging. In not truly seeing the other person, the one doing the judging becomes blind. Dietrich Bonhoeffer describes it this way: "Judging others makes us blind, whereas love is illuminating. By judging others we blind ourselves to our own evil and to the grace which others are just as entitled to as we are."[18] In the world of social psychology, this blindness is often identified as actor-observer bias, the human tendency to attribute our own circumstances and behaviors to external causes while attributing others' circumstances and behaviors to internal realities. A coworker gets a promotion you felt you deserved and expected, and your first thoughts are "I didn't get the promotion because the boss hates me" and "She got the promotion because she's willing to play office politics." This is actor-observer bias, and we judge others in this way a lot. We do it primarily for two reasons.

First, we do it to position ourselves over and above others. "I can't believe they did that / they're like that. What a mess. I would never..."

Second, we do it to protect ourselves from being exposed. "I can't believe they did that / they're like that. What a mess. At least I'm not..."

Both are, at their core, ways to conceal our real and whole selves from others and from ourselves. As a result, both are equally detrimental to meaningful connection and simultaneously vital to the survival of outrage and tribalism. Ultimately, both tendencies—to position ourselves and to protect ourselves—are tied to our shame. As Curt Thompson astutely points out, "The act of judging others has its origins in our self-judgment... 'Shamed people shame people.' Long before we are criticizing others, the source of that criticism has been planted, fertilized and grown in our own lives, directed at ourselves, and often in ways we are mostly unaware of."[19] We judge because we're ashamed. Put another way, outrage and tribalism cover a multitude of shame. But Jesus offers a way out from beneath the crushing weight of our shame.

> Do not judge, or you too will be judged. For in the same way you judge others, you will be judged, and with the measure you use, it will be measured to you. Why do you look at the speck of sawdust in your brother's eye and pay no attention to the plank in your own eye? How can you say to your brother, "Let me take the speck out of your eye," when all the time there is a plank in your own eye? (Matthew 7:1–4)

We don't often think of Jesus as funny, but he was.[20] A plank in the eye is a laughable and ludicrous image—intentionally so. Jesus is exposing the absolute absurdity of judgment. Judgment is ludicrous because all of us are living through the long arch of learning, growing, and changing. And to judge another person on that same journey simply because they are at a different point on that journey is to foolishly believe that we have somehow arrived when our own experiences make clear that there is and always will be so far to go. When we judge others, we are blind to the fact that our perspectives are just different. In his book *Humble*, social psychologist Daryl Van Tongeren writes that "once we change our viewpoint, we can't imagine why other people would be so foolish as to believe something different—even when we were those very same people in the recent past... Those who shift their ideological commitments roll their eyes at the ignorance of those who hold their previous beliefs. How quickly we forget how much we've learned, and how different we are now from what we once were. I can only imagine how incredibly annoyed I would be at myself ten, fifteen, or twenty years ago."[21]

When I'm painstakingly honest with myself, most of the time, the things that annoy or disturb me most about others is the stuff most inherently broken inside of me. In judging, I see red and am blind to both the existing pain and potential good in the other, as well as the existing brokenness and potential evil within myself.

But at this point, we're faced with a crucial question: What do we do with all of the actual brokenness in the world? Does acknowledgment of the plank in our eye lead to a different sort of blindness, toward the injustices, evils, and pain in our midst? "You hypocrite, first take the plank out of your own eye, and then you will see clearly *to remove the speck* from your brother's eye" (Matthew 7:5, emphasis added).

Taking the plank out of our own eye is not an invitation to turn a blind eye toward the wrong in our midst. It's the other way around. We take the plank out of our own eye in order that we might see clearly enough to join God in the work of setting wrong things right. This is what judgment at its finest is. Eugene Peterson reminds us, "Judgment is not a word about things, describing them; it is a word that does things, putting love in motion, applying mercy, nullifying wrong, ordering goodness."[22] When we're seeing red, we judge in order to position and protect ourselves at great expense to others, trampling and denigrating if necessary in order to hide in our shame. But when we begin to see clearly, judgment becomes an act of love, mercy, and goodness.

So how exactly do we begin to see clearly?

> For by the grace given me I say to every one of you: Do not think of yourself more highly than you ought, but rather think of yourself with sober judgment, in accordance with the faith God has distributed to each of you. For just as each of us has one body with many members, and these members do not all have the same function, so in Christ we, though many, form one body, and each member belongs to all the others. (Romans 12:3–5)

Seeing clearly begins with a "sober judgment" of ourselves. When we see red, when rage pushes us toward our tribes and we begin caricaturing those with whom we disagree, we take the plank out of our eye by taking a deep breath and praying even deeper prayers, asking God by his Spirit to ground us firmly in his peace and help us offer to others the patient grace he has so kindly offered to us. From there we recognize that we are all a part of the grand mess called humanity and that nothing is as black and white or us versus them as we might've assumed.

Sin is a complicated web of relationships where my wrongdoing has a direct effect on the wrong in the world. I am not without blame and "they" are not the enemy. We are all sinners saved by grace. This is what sober judgment of ourselves looks like. Dietrich Bonhoeffer summarizes the idea this way: "Christian love sees the fellow-man under the cross and therefore sees with clarity. If when we judged others, our real motive was to destroy evil, we should look for evil where it is certain to be found, and that is in our own hearts."[23]

Within the family of God, among Christian brothers and sisters, I am not my own. I belong to God, yes. But I also belong to the one I'm prone to judge. We are one body. My wrongdoing has a direct effect on others just as theirs has on me. *We* sin, *we* suffer, and by God's grace, *we* are saved. Recognizing our own contribution to the communal plight of human experience compels us to act, to remove planks and specks, and to work toward justice in the world, beginning right here before moving out there.

What Christians must combat most fiercely is blindness to evil in all forms and in all places—in them, in me, in us. The battle is not us versus them. It isn't my tribe against their tribe. It's the truth and grace and transformative power of

God against the evil forces of the enemy of God waging war against each and every human soul—yours, mine, ours.

In order to speak good news in an age of noise, we must first remove the planks from our eyes to see clearly. And as we do, our ears will follow suit, allowing us to not only see, but *hear*, the desperate longing to belong beneath the outrage and tribalism.

A RETURN TO CYNICISM

In my interactions with people in my church over the past few years, I've noticed a considerable uptick in cynicism. It's a cynicism that goes far beyond mere doubts about intentions or uncertainties about the future. As congregants in my church share their concerns about the present and future of their lives and our world, there is a growing sense that things simply are the way they are and that there's little to no chance of improvement in the foreseeable future. And what is more, there seems to be a growing cynicism about each other. We're losing hope in one another. We're cynical about people.

In the fifth century BC, there was a Greek philosopher named Diogenes who was born in Sinope, a city on the northern coast of modern-day Turkey. After being banished from his hometown for embezzling money, Diogenes landed in Athens, where he met Antisthenes, widely credited as the founder of the philosophical movement called cynicism.

Originally, the movement was much more than what comes to mind for us when we think of cynicism. A cynical person today is one who abides by a fixed set of beliefs regarding the irreversible depravity of humans and the hopelessness of life. But for Antisthenes, cynicism wasn't a set of beliefs; it was a particular way to exist in the world.

Antisthenes was frustrated by all the high-philosophy talk of his day, well-educated men bantering back and forth, waxing poetic about the various ills of the day and how enlightened people ought to think rightly about such matters. But as Antisthenes saw it, these men did very little in and with their actual lives to embody the principles and values they elucidated so eloquently with words. Diogenes, inspired by the teachings of Antisthenes, committed himself to a life of simplicity as a means of protest against the hypocrisy of Athenian high society. He spent many years living in a large clay pot on the streets of the city, surviving by begging.

According to a famous anecdote, one evening Diogenes was eating lentils, the food of the poor. A respected philosopher named Aristippus, who'd achieved comfort and wealth by aligning himself with the king, approached Diogenes and said, "If you would learn to be subservient to the king, you wouldn't have to live on lentils." Diogenes replied, "If you learned to live on lentils, you wouldn't have to be subservient to the king." Another story says that Diogenes one day wandered the streets of Athens at midday, holding a lantern

in broad daylight. When asked why he was doing such a preposterous thing, he replied, "I am looking for an honest man."

I share these stories to point out that cynicism at its roots
is not about a lack of hope or belief in better days ahead but
the opposite. Originally, the cynicism movement began as a
commitment to expose the falsehoods in our midst, to uncover
the hypocrisy and duplicity pervading culture and society, in
order to shed light on the truly worthwhile and meaningful,
and to work toward actual change in the world.

While the modern cynic is quickly dismissive, the ancient
cynic was disciplined and devout in his examination of any
and all matters before him. Or, as Arthur Brooks expounds,
"The modern cynic rejects things out of hand ('This is stupid'),
while the ancient cynic simply withholds judgment ('This may
be right or wrong')."[24] Modern cynicism is dangerous enough
when applied only to situations and circumstances, but it is
absolutely ruinous when applied, as it so often is, to other people. Outright rejection of one another widens the chasm that
already exists between us, further dividing us, more firmly
entrenching us in the depths of isolation, and dramatically
undermining our efforts to achieve what we long for most: to
be heard, to be seen, to be known, and to belong.

In the next few chapters, we'll explore ways that we can
begin to speak good news into the cacophony and chaos in
a way that cuts through the noise and is actually heard in a
meaningful way. But before we can speak good news, even

after we've attuned our ears to hear the voice of a God who sees us, we must also learn to hear the desire beneath the out- rage and tribalism. Such hearing requires a return to the roots of cynicism—but not the modern dismissive cynicism that caricatures people and writes them off as hopeless lost causes. Hearing clearly amid the outrage and tribalism demands a return to the sort of ancient cynicism that questions our own instinctual, reactive notions about others.

In his book *Uproar*, Peter Steinke writes that "until and unless you recognize the power of your own instinctual life, you will continue to assess outside conditions, persons, or ideas to be the cause of your or others' nervous unrest. So, in response, you use your energy to rectify, control, or elimi- nate the outside stimuli."[25] This is the cause of the destruction unfolding all around us, and even in us today. Our media- driven, algorithmically curated, reactive, shallow cynicism toward others is setting fire to potential paths toward belong- ing, and we are being pulled further and further apart, even though what we all long for is movement in the other direction.

Before we speak, we must learn to hear God and one another clearly.

And to hear one another clearly, we must see one another clearly, just as God sees us.

I wrote earlier about the pain of being judged in first grade as an immigrant outsider. But there was one saving grace that year. A few months into the school year, a tall, lanky, blond-haired, blue-eyed boy named Steven befriended me. We'd walk home the same way every day, and I eventually came to discover that we lived in the same apartment complex. An unlikely friendship formed. We overcame language and cultural barriers by way of a shared love for G.I. Joe and Transformers. We spent most weekday afternoons imagining adventures together. Steven was the only friend I made that entire first year of school. But he was all I needed. Though I was unseen by the rest, I was seen by one, and that's all it took.

I moved to another school in second grade, and that was the end of our friendship. I had to start over, several times. By the time fourth grade rolled around, I'd made a handful of friends and had a semblance of belonging at school for the first time in my life.

As it turns out, on the first day of fourth grade, I sat down at a desk next to a couple of my friends. A few moments later, a tall, lanky, blond-haired, blue-eyed boy walked into the classroom. He was new, and his demeanor bore the trademark nerves of an insecure kid unsure if he'd fit in. It was Steven. He was now the outsider.

At the first recess of the day, I walked over and introduced myself. He quickly recognized me. A relieved smile broke out on his face. My English was better now, and we enjoyed the pleasant surprise of more meaningful conversation. At lunch, I invited him to play kickball with me and my friends, our typical lunchtime ritual. He was immediately our best player.

We didn't lose that entire lunch period. Or ever. And it had nothing to do with the score.

We were together. We belonged.

We were seen and heard.

We couldn't lose.

PART II

Speak

Five

Why We Speak: Speaking Good News

For most of human history, news traveled as fast as transportation technology, and for many millennia this was only as fast as humans, with their own two feet, could walk or run. Then came horseback and eventually ships and trains. But in the mid-nineteenth century, Samuel Morse developed the first telegraph machine along with Morse code, and everything changed. News could now travel at the speed of electrical signals sent over wire.

Morse sent the very first telegraph message in 1844, between Washington, DC, and Baltimore. It read, "What hath God wrought?"—but it's unlikely he knew just how prescient that question was. By 1866, a wire had been laid across the Atlantic, enabling telegraph communication between the United States and Europe. The technology eventually gave way to the telephone, radio, television, and the internet, which further sped the travel of news, irreversibly and forever. In so doing, these technologies dramatically also changed the *nature* of news.

Before the telegraph, telephone, radio, television, and the internet, news was almost exclusively local. What was happening at the moment in Europe mattered very little to those living in Asia, because by the time word was able to get from one part of the world to the other, it was old news. It was of no consequence. As such, news was overwhelmingly practical—intended to be practically informative, practically helpful, and practically applied to the immediate circumstances at hand. In other words, news was always about subjects that had a direct effect on people's actual lives. The intent and purpose of news was to affect and influence what people could and should do in light of the information, not how people could or should opine, comment, or critique.

The twentieth-century author and cultural critic Neil Postman wrote that the telegraph "gave a form of legitimacy to the idea of context-free information; that is, to the idea that the value of information need not be tied to any function it might serve."[1] Eventually successors to the telegraph, like the television, he writes, "made information into a commodity, a 'thing' that could be bought and sold irrespective of its uses or meaning." We only need to scroll Twitter or the news app feeds on our phones for a few brief moments to know just how much this information-as-commodity, nonfunctional (one could argue dysfunctional) reality has been accelerated in the digital age.

The news is no longer about what's happened here, informing us what we should do about it now. The news is now mostly about what's happening there and everywhere, and how we should opine, comment, and critique—immediately and all at once. Postman's prescient words from a 1990 speech articulate well our current condition: "The tie between information and action has been severed. Information is now... a form of entertainment, or worn like a garment to enhance one's status...we are glutted with information, drowning in information, have no control over it, don't know what to do with it."[2]

Speaking into such an environment is no doubt extremely challenging. But for followers of Jesus, recapturing the gospel in both speech and embodied action offers a tailor-made opportunity to be heard in a noisy world.

GOOD NEWS

The word *gospel* comes from the Greek word *euangelion*, which was originally a political term used by the Roman Empire. At the time of Jesus, whenever Caesar's armies would defeat an enemy and conquer a new land, a herald would ceremoniously proclaim the *euangelion* of Caesar—that Rome had triumphed once again, that a new era of peace and prosperity would be ushered into this freshly decimated territory, and that the greatness of the empire was expanding. All of this was "good news."

After the death, resurrection, and ascension of Jesus, the first Christians co-opted this political term and began using

it to proclaim his victory, not over people, land, and territory, but over sin and death: "The *gospel* of God—the *gospel*
he promised beforehand through his prophets in the Holy
Scriptures regarding his Son, who as to his earthly life was
a descendant of David, and who through the Spirit of holi-
ness was appointed the Son of God in power by his resurrection from the dead: Jesus Christ our Lord" (Romans 1:1–4,
emphasis added).

Jesus Christ our Lord. The Christians claimed that it was
Jesus, not Caesar, who truly ruled the world and that this was
the real good news. As N. T. Wright puts it: "The Christian
faith, in its earliest forms, is presented as good news."[3]

Sadly, most modern Christians misunderstand faith as a
primarily intellectual exercise, a mental ascent toward a set of
ideas and beliefs. This isn't untrue; it's just incomplete. The
Greek word for "faith" is *pistis*, and though its most accurate
meaning is somewhat debated, there is widespread agreement
among scholars that it means much more than intellectual
belief. Biblically speaking, faith is best understood as trust,
loyalty, or allegiance in another person rather than a set of
ideas or ideologies we hold on to for ourselves.

But because the Christian faith is often rendered as a set
of dogmas—instead of a trust in Jesus—the interpretation and
application of these dogmas have become the meaning of *gospel* to many. As such, differences in particular interpretations
and applications of the gospel have created spiteful division

among Christians. Rather than expressing the good news of Jesus as Jesus would—with clarity and conviction expressed in love and grace—many wield their beliefs as weapons to tear down any and all who might disagree. As a result, the public witness of the church has suffered a great deal, as many Christians so often seem far more interested in winning arguments over cultural issues and making social commentary. We hurl dismissive barbs rather than point to good news, and this is the natural consequence of misunderstanding the nature of the gospel. In recent years, on Twitter alone, I've read that the gospel is, in no particular order, the following:

- Care for the poor, oppressed, and marginalized in our midst.
- Upholding the sanctity of life and protecting the pro-life position.
- Racial reconciliation.
- Immigration reform.
- Gun reform.
- Economic reform.
- Climate reform.

To be clear, these are vitally important issues that the Bible has much to say about. I would wholeheartedly agree that the gospel informs, affects, and can absolutely redeem all of the brokenness these particular issues and more seek to address.

These are not unimportant matters. They are important—critically so. But they are not in and of themselves the gospel. By definition, they can't be. Because the gospel is good *news*.

News isn't about what should happen. News is, by definition, something that's already happened that directly affects the present and the future. The gospel then is the news that two thousand years ago a Jewish rabbi in the Middle East claimed to be God, was then crucified and killed and buried, only to rise again three days later, before eventually ascending to heaven as the rightful king of the universe, promising to return someday to fully and totally actualize and realize his kingdom on earth as it is in heaven. *That's* the Gospel, the good news of what's happened, which changes everything, today and forever.

But of course the gospel isn't just news; it's *good* news. It's important to remember that *good news* doesn't necessarily mean every problem is fixed and every pain healed immediately. For many years of my life, I dealt with significant pain on the sole of my right foot. It would come and go, but at times it was debilitating. One painful episode left me unable to walk for a couple of days and eventually put me in a walking boot.

After years of ignoring it and hoping it'd just go away, I finally went to the podiatrist for an examination. X-rays revealed that two small bones were fused together in a way they shouldn't be, suggesting that the condition was very likely genetic. The doctor gave me a few exercises and stretches to do, a prescription for a minor anti-inflammatory, and said that surgery could be an option in the future but wasn't necessary now. He concluded, "This is good news."

The diagnosis wasn't good news because I was out of the woods and the bones had magically healed. Reaggravation is still a constant risk. I have to be careful about how much pressure I put on the foot, and I'm limited in the sorts of motions I can make. No, the diagnosis was good news because the problem and the path ahead had both been clearly identified. It's good news because I'm informed, I can do something about it, and I have help. It's good news because how I respond to it can have a significantly positive effect on both my present and my future.

The gospel doesn't mean everything's going to feel good right now. It doesn't mean immediate and total relief for all that ails us in this life. But the gospel is inherently and eternally good. It informs us accurately of the human condition, diagnosing our sin and offering a path toward salvation, healing, and wholeness. The good news is that a path has been laid and a price has been paid, and we don't have to wonder anymore if things will someday be made right. We know they will be.

As the world busies itself with commentary and critique on news that doesn't really matter, followers of Jesus are called to speak truly good news, the story of something that's already happened and that changes everything now and forever, offering a way out of the mess we find ourselves in. And to do this effectively, we begin with distress and reason.

DISTRESS AND REASON

In Acts 17, the apostle Paul is in the city of Athens. At the time, though, the city was no longer the epicenter of the known world as it was several hundreds of years earlier, Athens remained a highly influential city, full of commerce, high art, and intellectual innovation. Much religious and philosophical thought was still birthed there, and the city valued both rhetoric and debate. But as he awaits his friends Silas and Timothy, Paul is overwhelmed by the idolatrous spiritual and cultural climate.

In response, he begins to preach the gospel in the local synagogue and in the marketplace, two of the major centers of community life in the city. In essence, Paul takes the good news to the places where people are. Eventually, "a group of Epicurean and Stoic philosophers began to debate with him" (Acts 17:18), and they lead him up to "a meeting of the Areopagus" (v. 19).

Named after the Greek god of war, Ares (Mars in Latin, thus the moniker Mars Hill), this rocky outcropping in Athens sat several hundred feet above ground, and it's where the Areopagus Council, a group of leaders who presided over court cases in the city, met. The Greek philosophers bring

Paul to this legal court of law because, in their estimation, he was "bringing some strange ideas to our ears, and we would like to know what they mean" (Acts 17:20). The philosophers intend to dissect, pull apart, and deconstruct this outsider's message. This is, after all, the Athenian idea of a good time: "All the Athenians and the foreigners who lived there spent their time doing nothing but talking about and listening to the latest ideas" (v. 21). Paul goes on to deliver one of the New Testament's most compelling and captivating Gospel sermons (vv. 22–31).

But all of this begins for Paul with a surprising paradox. Upon seeing the spirit of idolatry running rampant throughout Athens, Paul "was greatly *distressed*" (Acts 17:16, emphasis added), so "he *reasoned*" (v. 17, emphasis added) with people in the synagogue, in the marketplace, and eventually at the Areopagus.

Distress. A deep provocation of the soul. An unrest and angst because of things not being as they should be.

Reason. A tempered and clear response, built not on hype and hyperbole but on steadiness and calm conviction.

Distress and reason. The two don't typically go together. In an age of clickbait headlines, soundbites, pundits, personalities, and influencers, they almost never go together.

Distress begets lots of things: indignation, outrage, chaos, uproar, shouting down, screaming out. But reason? No. Almost never.

Yet that's exactly what Paul does. And it's exactly what

effectively speaking good news looks like today. The verse immediately following Paul's distress and reason tells us that he was *"preaching* the good news about Jesus and the resurrection" (Acts 17:18, emphasis added). The word *preaching* here is the verb form of the Greek word *euangelion*, gospel. Paul is *gospeling*, quite literally the definition of *speaking good news*.

Paul is *distressed* by the surrounding sin, idolatry, and brokenness.

Paul *reasons* with calm conviction, no hype, no hyperbole.

Paul *gospels*—he speaks the good news.

This is the blueprint. Speaking good news in such a way that we might be heard begins first with distress. We identify, acknowledge, confess, and repent of the idolatry in our midst—first in our own hearts, minds, and lives, and then in the surrounding culture.

In February 2023, a small chapel service at Asbury University in Wilmore, Kentucky, extended beyond its end time. For over a week, students, faculty, and eventually tens of thousands of visitors from all over the world gathered to worship, pray, and seek God together. Some called it the Asbury Awakening. Almost all who attended noted two distinguishing characteristics.

First was the fact that it all seemed to begin with corporate confession and repentance. Story after story of students confessing and repenting of individual and corporate sins began spilling out of Asbury, and the world took notice. Pastor Jon

Tyson shared a video of a young man publicly repenting sin and giving his life to Christ, with the congregation erupting in applause.[4] This sort of scene was common during the revival. The loudest cheers were not reserved for songs and sermons but primarily for the moments when people brought hidden brokenness into the light. A culture exhausted by hyperbole and manufactured fanfare was captivated by the simple beauty and humble potency of young people surrendering to Christ. Distress was at the center of it all.

The second distinguishing characteristic was the noticeable lack of hype, gimmickry, and Christian celebrity. As the gathering grew, the city of Wilmore (population 6,000) was overwhelmed with people flooding in from far and wide to witness the event. This was an opportune moment to highlight the greatness of the university and leverage the movement of God in a way that would benefit the school. But the leaders of Asbury were clear: they wanted the revival to remain "nameless and faceless."[5]

Zach Meerkreebs, a volunteer soccer coach at Asbury, had delivered the sermon at the initial chapel service. After he finished, he thought that he'd "totally whiffed," texting his wife, "Latest stinker. I'll be home soon."[6] But God used the sermon of a volunteer—not the chaplain, not a mega-pastor or prominent leader—to do incredible things those few weeks. The Asbury Awakening wasn't about bright lights and big names. It was tempered and calm and steady. It was *reasonable*.

Distress and reason. Like coming up for breath after being caught for too long in an undertow, moments like the Asbury Awakening remind us that what truly captures listening ears, inquisitive minds, and open hearts in a world of noise is not more of the same. It's not the hype machine building up polished brands that seemingly have it all together. It's genuine distress—humility, confession, repentance. And it's the voice of reason—tempered and steady, calm and convicted, sober and clear.

Not all who heard Paul speaking the good news at Mars Hill were convinced. Some "sneered" (Acts 17:32). But some believed, including a member of the Areopagus Council named Dionysius. Tradition tells us that Dionysius was baptized by Paul, who appointed him as the leader of the Christian movement in Athens. Dionysius would then take the good news to Gaul, known at the time to be a dangerous and barbaric place, before he was martyred for his faith in AD 96 under the reign of the Roman emperor Domitian.

Moved to distress and led by reason, Paul speaks the good news in idolatrous Athens and it changes Dionysius's life, leading him to continue speaking the good news to parts of the world Paul would never see. This same sort of opportunity is at hand for followers of Jesus today.

I was a bit of a hellion in my early teens. My freshman year of high school, short on cash, as most teenagers are, I started shoplifting cartons of cigarettes from a local store and selling them out of my school locker. The money was nice and the notoriety of being the local smoke shop felt good for my fragile, insecure ego. Then I got caught.

The store soon realized that this skinny teenager always walking in and out and wearing a thick parka in the warm California sun and never actually buying anything was a bit suspicious. One afternoon, an undercover security guard followed me out, sternly grabbed my shoulder, and opened up my jacket, and a carton of Camels fell right out.

About a month later, I found myself in juvenile court. Saved from a harsher sentence by my mother's pleas for leniency, the judge gave me six months of community service. I was required to volunteer at a local garden every afternoon for the remainder of the school year and into the summer. A retired woman named Lori ran the garden, and though she knew I was there as part of a court-mandated program, she was nothing but kind and compassionate toward me.

Rather than keep me at a defensive distance, Lori extended me the gift of empathy, taking a genuine interest in me and my story.

Rather than seeing me as a bad kid beyond saving, she chose to see me as a good kid in need of direction, discipline, and care.

Recognizing the distress in my life, Lori empathized.

And her reasoned approach came across as goodness.

Empathy and goodness.

Lori embodied and modeled these gifts for me during a dark and confusing time of life. And I heard her. I heard her in a way I hadn't heard others before. Followers of Jesus can and must speak in the same way today if we want to be heard. This is what the good news sounds like in a noisy world.

SUPERNATURAL EMPATHY

I've been told that the things that grate on us most about our children are their traits and tendencies that resemble us most. I don't know how true this is generally, but I know it's irrefutably true for me and my kids. Especially with my son, I find myself most irritable and short tempered when he reflects my own shortcomings and deficiencies.

When he was four, Simon went through many long months of a hellaciously temperamental appetite. He refused to eat anything that wasn't perfectly to his liking. Sometimes if a piece of food wasn't placed in his bowl just so, he'd toss it aside in a crying rage. Then one day, this daily meltdown unfolded while my mother was over for dinner. She said to Simon (and, I think, a little bit to me), "Oh, your daddy used to do exactly that when he was your age."

For weeks after, any and every time I lost my temper at his pickiness over food, Simon would suddenly calm down and say to me, "I'm just like you, Daddy. I'm just like you." Yes you are, son.

This uncomfortable revelation, that my son was temperamental just like me, became an unexpected catalyst for renewed empathy toward my little boy. I found myself growing just a little bit slower to anger and a little bit more abounding in love. I began owning, and even appreciating, the slices of the big personality in this little human that came from me. And slowly things began to change. My son grew a bit more resilient as he felt better understood and less alone in his frustrations. My furious scolding never seemed to register with him, but almost miraculously, my patient empathy caught his ear. He began hearing me.

The author of Hebrews reminds us that Jesus is a very specific sort of great high priest:

> We do not have a high priest who is unable to *empathize* with our weaknesses, but we have one who has been tempted in every way, just as we are—yet he did not sin. Let us then approach God's throne of grace with confidence, so that we may receive mercy and find grace to help us in our time of need. (Hebrews 4:15–16, emphasis added)

The word *empathize* is the translation of the Greek word *synpatheo*, which combines two words and literally means "to suffer with." Forget for a moment what you know of the cross and the crucifixion of Christ. One would assume the exact opposite of this text. If God took on flesh and entered the human story to redeem it, we'd expect him to come in strength and vitality, not suffer. First-century Jews certainly had this expectation of the coming Messiah.

Jesus was not the sort of Messiah anyone expected; he eschewed the superhero's cape for the criminal's crown. But the Jewish people should have known better, and so should we. It was prophesied long ago, after all, that the Messiah would have "no beauty of majesty to attract us to him, nothing in his appearance that we should desire him" (Isaiah 53:2). He'd be "despised and rejected by mankind, a man of suffering, and familiar with pain" (v. 3).

Jesus empathizes not with our successes and strengths, but with our weaknesses. He knows suffering and pain. The sinless one knows what could not be further from his nature. He lays himself down in order to be raised up. He surrenders in order to ascend. He dies in order to live. This is the way of Jesus. And this is the way to speak good news today.

In his letter to the Romans, the apostle Paul writes, "Bless those who persecute you; bless and do not curse. Rejoice with those who rejoice; mourn with those who mourn. Live in harmony with one another. Do not be proud, but be willing to associate with people of low position. Do not be conceited" (Romans 12:14–16). In a world constantly incensed at slights big and small, Christians are to be a peculiar people who bless instead of curse. While the world rejoices when their enemies mourn and mourns when their enemies rejoice, followers of

Jesus rejoice with the rejoicing and mourn with the mourning, surrendering our pride and bending down to draw near the lowly, just as Christ bent down toward us.

This is the way to be heard. But it's impossible without help.

Defensiveness, cynicism, and hostility are all natural to humans. But the sort of empathy that can overcome these natural tendencies is supernatural. It's only possible when God, by his Spirit, forms us into Christlikeness, slowly over time, as we surrender our privileges and preferences for the sake of others. Paul describes the process in his letter to the Philippians: "In humility value others above yourselves, not looking to your own interests but each of you to the interests of the others. In your relationships with one another, have the same mindset as Christ Jesus" (Philippians 2:3–5).

Having the "same mindset as Christ" is beyond human ability. Theologian Gordon Fee explains that the "ultimate paradigm of a genuinely Christian mindset is Christ himself, who is the premier manifestation of the character of God, which God is trying to reproduce in his people."[7] God himself produces in us the very likeness of his son. This isn't to say we do nothing. Far from it. We must do the daily work of dying to ourselves and bending our will around his.

As we do, we will over time become the sorts of people who embody and reflect the jarring, countercultural humility of Christ, "Who, being in very nature God, did not consider equality with God something to be used to his own advantage; rather, he made himself nothing by taking the very nature of a servant, being made in human likeness. And being found in appearance as a man, he humbled himself by becoming obedient to death—even death on a cross!" (Philippians 2:6–8).

What does this look like with regard to speaking good news in a noisy world? Over the course of two decades of pastoring, I've found two specific statements considerably helpful in expressing humility, even in tense and potentially hostile or divisive conversations:

I'm sorry.
Tell me more.

Some linguists think that the word *sorry* originates from the old Norse word *sarr*, meaning "sore or wound," which led to an Old English word, *sar*, meaning "painful, aching, wounding," which then eventually gave way to the more modern words *sore* and *sorrow*. We typically think of *I'm sorry* as a personal apology, which it is, of course. But these two simple words also convey empathy. It's a way of leaning into the pain, ache, and wound of another. In a noisy world, we've come to believe that every action, especially opposition or antagonism, demands and deserves a firm reaction. Sometimes this is true. But often, saying *I'm sorry* as a way of communicating "I see and hold your pain, ache, and wound with you" is a powerful and effective way to be heard.

Once common ground has been laid through empathy, curiosity must lead the way. On the surface this might seem counterintuitive. Being heard is about speaking, not listening. But *Tell me more* is one of the most universally effective ways to engage the mind and heart of another.

My friend Steve Carter writes about the need to grow in awareness of what he calls "the thing beneath the thing," which he describes as the "deep, dark places hidden away in [the] deep crevices of [our] soul(s)."[8] What's on the surface—anger, vitriol, outrage, and so on—is almost never what's actually in the depths. Deep beneath the surface are the hidden complexities, nuances, and layers of our personal histories, stories of success and failure, disappointment, uncertainty, and all the rest. What looks like anger, vitriol, and outrage on the surface is almost always some form of pain, fear, and anxiety beneath.

Tell me more is a way of helping excavate deeper, finding a truly meaningful connection. It's here, in the "deep, dark places hidden away" that the noise quiets enough for us to finally speak with truth, love, grace, and the rest.

A few years ago, my wife, Jenny, and I were shopping at a local store when we heard yelling a few aisles down. We made our way over to find a young man in his twenties babbling loudly and incoherently to himself. A store employee and a few well-meaning customers tried to intervene, but none seemed to be able to get through to the man. He was clearly in distress but struggling to communicate why. Because my wife is a special education teacher, she had some familiarity with young people on the severe end of the autism spectrum.

Jenny gently made her way over to him and spoke quietly. He eventually shared his name and a few other bits of information I couldn't make out. I heard Jenny then say, "I'm sorry," and "Tell me more." A calm relief came over the young man, and eventually we were able to reach his caretaker on the phone. High tension gave way to the safety and peace of empathy.

I'm sorry and *Tell me more.*

No five words might be better heard in a noisy world.

SEEING BEFORE SPEAKING GOODNESS

In 1889, Vincent van Gogh sold a painting called *The Red Vineyard* to a Belgian art collector named Anna Boch for

400 francs, the equivalent of about $1,000 today. Though art historians argue that van Gogh might've sold a few other paintings, most likely a handful of small portraits, *The Red Vineyard* is the only painting for which we have a record of a sale during his lifetime. Today, his collection of paintings has an estimated value in the tens of billions of dollars. How does a master like Vincent van Gogh go so dramatically under-appreciated in his lifetime?

Seeing the good in something (or someone) isn't always easy. But it is possible. In fact recognizing the *possibility* of goodness in others is the key to seeing their goodness. Think about the life of first-time parents. I remember the sleepless nights and extreme exhaustion of those early months after our daughter was born. We'd never loved another human quite like this before, but taking care of her was more than we'd bargained for. Harper was a fussy baby, always needing to be held, waking up countless times throughout the night. And while she doesn't need us to rock her back to sleep anymore, objectively speaking, she still takes far more than she gives. So does our son.

They don't pay rent, but they always have a place to sleep.

They don't pitch in for groceries, but they always have food to eat.

They don't do laundry, but they always have clean clothes to wear.

They don't contribute much on paper, but they consume a ton.

Why do Jenny and I put up with it? First and foremost because of love. Our kids are infinitely valuable. But also because of possibility. We gladly love into this inequity because we hope that someday they will grow to be people who embody and express the love they've received, from God and from their parents, and then in turn love God and those around them. We don't know that any of this will happen. There's no guarantee. But it's our hope. And hopeful possibility is enough. It's enough to help us see the good in them now, more often than not.

To speak good news in a noisy world, we must see the possible good within those we engage with, which in turn helps us to see the good in them now. Even amid great tension, disagreement, and hostility, those who speak good news must learn to see any perceived foolishness of others not as a fixed reality but as a temporary stop on the journey of growth, a stop we've all visited countless times in our own lives. To do so also demands acknowledgment of our own past and present foolishness. Speaking good news begins on even ground, where we are all sinners in need of grace. And this even ground reveals itself to be solid ground, built on Christ our cornerstone, who does indeed save us from our sin and our foolishness.

The apostle Paul writes early on in his first letter to the Corinthian church that "the message of the cross is foolishness to those who are perishing, but to us who are being saved it is the power of God" (1 Corinthians 1:18). From passages like this, we typically divide everyone up into two groups. There are the perishing and there are the saved. But the whole point of the gospel is that those who are perishing, as we all once were, can become the saved. This means that foolishness is brimming with the potential for power. It is an indefensible contradiction to believe this to be true in our journey from perishing to saved but not true for others on the same journey.

The fork in the road where the paths of foolishness and power diverge is marked by two distinct stories. We must choose to embrace, embody, strive toward, and speak one of the two.

The first story is the story of self-sufficiency. It's the story that our culture has titled *I am enough*. But the biblical story makes clear this is a lie. As Paul writes, "[Jesus] said to me, 'My grace is sufficient for you, for my power is made perfect in weakness.' Therefore I will boast all the more gladly about my weaknesses, so that Christ's power may rest on me. That is why, for Christ's sake, I delight in weaknesses, in insults, in hardships, in persecutions, in difficulties. For when I am weak, then I am strong" (2 Corinthians 12:9–10). We are not enough. This isn't to say you and I are not loved. We are, more than we can possibly know. But we are loved in spite of our depravity, not because of our sufficiency. This is what makes love of any kind so profound and compelling: it comes to us as an undeserved gift, not as an earned, rightly owed compensation.

The second story is the story of God's sufficiency. It's the story of Jesus, descending into the mess of humanity, descending even further into the depths of death, and rising again, having mortally wounded the grave, and ascending to the throne as the king of the universe. It's the gospel story. It's the good news story we've been given, in order to tell it to the world. This story stands in stark opposition to the first story and confronts the various false narratives of our age.

Seeing the good in one another isn't so much about seeing the inherent good (though it's there, to be sure) but rather about seeing the potential of the goodness of God rewriting each of our stories. This is God's grace.

Tim Keller, writing about the surprising and incredible effectiveness of his church's ministry in a post-Christian Manhattan in the early years after planting, said, "Looking back on that time, the most important reason for this was that we were offering God's grace as a unique path, different from either religious moralism or secular relativism. And going forward, a renewed Christian Church must focus on this identity-altering, life-changing, community-forming message in the same way."[9]

The unique path of God's grace—that he is rewriting our stories—is different from the path of self-sufficiency that so many traverse in our day and age, and it is the one and only way out of foolishness and into the saving power of the gospel. The most effective way to invite people to journey down that path is by seeing in them their goodness of course but more importantly the good that God can do in and through them. Any message other than the message of God's grace simply adds to the noise.

Speaking with clarity and conviction about a singular path forward is of course offensive in our pluralistic world. This is why our distress must always express itself reasonably. In his book *Good Arguments*, world champion debater Bo Seo talks about the importance of "revealing the journey" when arguing for a particular view or perspective. He writes, "Besides explaining *what* you believe and *why*, tell the story of *how* you came to believe it. Listeners often find the prospect of changing their mind to be terrifying. They want to know where the speaker is coming from, so that they may be able to trust and even identify with the person."[10]

Revealing our journey humanizes the situation and situates our ideas within the context of a story. Speaking good news in a world overrun by noisy ideas and ideologies comes most alive when told as the greatest story among a litany of lesser stories. And the stories we tell, believe, and live are the stories we become.

Between July and November 1916, more than three million soldiers fought at the Battle of Somme, one of the deadliest battles in World War I and in all of human history. When all was said and done, one million men were either wounded or killed. Two young soldiers in particular fought on opposing sides during those months in France. A twenty-seven-year-old soldier named Adolf Hitler fought for the Germans, while a twenty-four-year-old named John Ronald Reuel Tolkien fought for the Allied forces.

Hitler and Tolkien both experienced the same brutal atrocities at Somme. They buried friends and wondered if they'd make it out alive. Eventually both young men made their ways back home, irreparably changed. But they responded in different ways.

Adolf Hitler imagined a world where his version of good could overcome his version of evil. He believed that the enemy were those who were different from himself, and he believed this to the point of dehumanizing the other, fooling himself into seeing them as less than totally human. The cross was indeed foolishness to him. Why die for the worthless when you could simply eliminate them? He gave the rest of his life to eradicating these enemies in an attempt to create his good new world, relying on self-sufficiency. This led to World War II and the Holocaust.

J. R. R. Tolkien also imagined a world where good would overcome evil. And despite experiencing the worst of human beings at the Battle of Somme, he knew that the true enemy was not natural but supernatural. Tolkien believed that there was a deeper and truer story taking place on the battlefield of war and the battlefield of life itself. Though he'd taken up arms against his fellow man and his fellow man against him, his Christian faith taught him that something more sinister was beneath the surface but there was a way out, a better story unfolding in ways we often miss. This led him to write the Lord of the Rings saga.

In *The Fellowship of the Ring*, the first book of the trilogy, the wise wizard Gandalf tells the protagonist Frodo, "There are other forces at work in this world, Frodo, besides the will of evil."[11] Yes, there are. Despite the evil in the world and the brokenness in us, there are other forces at work. Ever since sin marred the human story, God has been authoring a new story. The first and last words have already been written. It's the story that followers of Jesus have been reading, living, and proclaiming for generations. It's the story we have to tell, a good news story for a noisy world.

Six

How We Speak: Speaking Biblically

In my very early years as a pastor, I was asked to visit with an elderly man in our congregation who was in his last days. The family wanted me to spend some time with him, and I was honored to do so. But this being one of the first times I'd pastored someone nearing death, I was racked with anxiety. In the hours leading up to my visit, I found myself scrambling to formulate something to say that would be meaningful and comforting. Bible verses, seminary studies on eschatology and the afterlife, and pithy pastoral tidbits rushed across my mental landscape.

When I arrived, the family welcomed me with kind and somber smiles, and I made my way toward Earl's bedside. After taking a quiet breath, I began talking. But just a few sentences in, he shushed me gently.

"Just read me the psalms, Jay."

Earl didn't want my theological commentary or my well-crafted words of comfort. He wanted the Scriptures. And I was relieved. I opened my Bible and began reading the psalms, just as he asked. Eventually I made my way to Psalm 119 and this verse: "Your word is a lamp for my feet, a light on my path" (v. 105).

That was it. I read for almost an hour and said no more than a dozen words of my own to Earl. And it was more than enough. As he navigated the end of one life and the start of eternal life, my friend wanted the Bible to light the path before him, the path to heaven. In the coldest and darkest moments, the warmest light is often the light of Scripture.

Six hundred years before the birth of Christ, a man named Ezekiel had an ecstatic vision of heaven and heard God calling him to prophetically speak on his behalf to his people. He recollected his experience this way:

> Then I looked, and I saw a hand stretched out to me. In it was a scroll, which he unrolled before me. On both sides of it were written words of lament and mourning and woe. And he said to me, "Son of man, eat what is before you, eat this scroll; then go and speak to the people of Israel." So I opened my mouth, and he gave me the scroll to eat. Then he said to me, "Son of man, eat this scroll I am giving you and fill your stomach with it." So I ate it, and it tasted as sweet as honey in my mouth. He then said to me: "Son of man, go now to the people of Israel and speak my words to them." (Ezekiel 2:9–3:4)

Before sending Ezekiel to speak, God instructs him to eat: *Eat this scroll, then go and speak.* We'd be wise in our day and age to heed these words. In chapter 2 we examined the sustaining nature of the Bible as our daily bread. But it only sustains us if and when we consume it. The Bible on the shelf leaves us spiritually famished just as bread on the counter leaves us physically hungry. But as Scripture becomes our sustenance, it can then become the source of our words and the gift of good news we offer to a spiritually starving world. But we face unique challenges to speaking biblically today.

THE OFFENSE OF SCRIPTURE

On January 13, 2023, pastor and author Tim Keller tweeted, "Nothing more important for a Christian to do than to read right through the whole Bible over and over and over, at the very least once a year. You have to keep checking and refining your beliefs by immersion in the Scripture."[1] As is typical for most tweets by people with a large public platform, Keller's tweet was met with a mix of mostly positive affirmations alongside a fair share of enraged critiques. One response was especially scathing. A few hours after the original tweet, the writer David Dark responded, "This is the language of spiritual abuse."[2] In further responses, Dark cited an interview in which he defines spiritual abuse this way:

> I think plain old abuse becomes spiritual abuse the moment I speak or act as if I'm an authority in someone else's experience. It's a refusal to honor another person's

boundaries because I believe (or wish to imply) that I'm closer to God or more intimately familiar with God's purposes than someone else. It's a form of violence, whether in speech or behavior, in which I try to deny someone the right to assess their own thoughts, feelings or experiences without me.[3]

Keller was a professed Christian primarily speaking to other Christians. It's fair enough to argue the merits of his suggestion that there's "nothing more important" for a Christian than to read the Bible over and over again. Calling Keller's assertion wrong, misguided, or incomplete would make sense, depending on one's particular view of how lives are most effectively formed into Christlikeness. But to call it "spiritual abuse," defined as "violence," is telling.

Every month, our church hosts a small gathering for people who are new to our community. A significant part of our time together is an open question and response session. In the past couple of years, every time, without fail, we've had at least a handful of people ask questions about accountability systems within our church leadership structure. The increased desire for transparency has been noticeable.

Most of these questions most of the time are born out of deep hurt and, in some cases, trauma from past church experiences in which spiritual authority was abused. We consider it a significant responsibility and vitally important work to listen to these victims and provide what support we can to help those hurting find the necessary space to grieve, question, doubt, and heal, and to do so with others when ready. Spiritual abuse is real, it's not the way of Jesus, and I grieve its existence.

But going back for a moment to David Dark's definition of *abuse*, if Keller's tweet encouraging Christians to read the Bible denies them "the right to assess their own thoughts, feelings or experiences," then does all encouragement or advice deny others this right? How would we distinguish between any advice and abuse?

Imagine if Stephen Curry tweeted, "Nothing more important for a hooper to do than to shoot 500 shots a day, over and over and over. You have to keep checking and refining your mechanics." Or if a prolific author tweeted, "Nothing more important for a writer to do than read broadly and write consistently, every day, over and over and over. You have to keep checking and refining your thoughts and words." Or if a Michelin Star chef tweeted, "Nothing more important for a cook to do than to cook and cook and cook some more, every day. You have to keep checking and refining your skill and creativity."

My guess is that no one would bat an eye. Many would applaud and affirm. Some would beg to differ, saying that other practices might be more important for basketball players, writers, and chefs. And all of it would be fair. But it's difficult to imagine, even in our hypersensitive culture, that anyone would credibly call it abuse, whether "plain old" or "spiritual" in nature.

Skilled practitioners share their opinions all the time about what had an impact on their development and can have, in their estimation, on the development of others. While disagreements are common, accusations of abuse are unheard of. My sense is that the firestorm on Twitter over Keller's tweet involved something more than just warring definitions of *abuse* or animosity toward Keller. In part, the tweet elicited the response it did because Scripture, and its self-proclaimed authority, is an offense.

THE OFFENSE OF AUTHORITY

Secular culture's default posture toward the Bible is typically either disinterest at best or disgust at worst. Richard Dawkins's now famous indictment of the God of the Bible is more and more the accepted view: "The God of the Old Testament is arguably the most unpleasant character in all fiction: jealous and proud of it; a petty, unjust, unforgiving control-freak; a vindictive, bloodthirsty ethnic cleanser; a misogynistic, homophobic, racist...bully."[4] As a follower of Jesus whose life has been radically transformed by the Scriptures, I'd disagree. But for the sake of this book, that's neither here nor there. The point is that it's difficult to speak biblically today because the operating system of culture assumes that the Bible is misogynistic, homophobic, racist, and so on. This is no way to be heard.

But how does the Bible describe the Bible?

All Scripture is God-breathed. (2 Timothy 3:16)

Everything that was written in the past was written to teach us, so that through the endurance taught in the Scriptures and the encouragement they provide we might have hope. (Romans 15:4)

Heaven and earth will pass away, but my words will never pass away. (Matthew 24:35)

My word that goes out from my mouth; it will not return to me empty, but will accomplish what I desire and achieve the purpose for which I sent it. (Isaiah 55:11)

The early church fathers echoed these authoritative truths regarding Scripture.[5]

Irenaeus (130–202): "By the will of God, they delivered to us in the Scriptures, to be for the future the foundation and pillar of our faith."

Athanasius (300–375): "The Holy Scriptures, given by inspiration of God, are of themselves sufficient toward the discovery of truth."

Cyril of Jerusalem (315–386): "The security and preservation of our faith are not supported by ingenuity of speech, but by the proofs of the divine Scriptures."

For Christians, these words are comforting. But one can see how an unbelieving world would take offense. Such explicit and definitive statements of authority, from the Bible or any other source, have little chance of gaining a hearing in the anti-authoritarian climate of our day.

In January 2023, Rabbi Joshua Franklin stood in front of the congregation he serves at the Jewish Center of the Hamptons and delivered a thousand-word sermon on intimacy and vulnerability. Surprisingly, he noted early on that the sermon was plagiarized. But by the end of the sermon, the congregation was applauding. It was that good. Rabbi Franklin revealed that the sermon had been written by ChatGPT, the artificial intelligence program developed by OpenAI.

The story received national attention. Was this the end of original content from clergy? Could AI be in the early stages of upending humans as spiritual leaders? There's a lot of discussion these days about the rise of AI and what it might mean for the present and the future. But I share this story only to point out how AI can erode trust at the most fundamental human levels.

I didn't use ChatGPT or any other AI platform to write this book. These thoughts and words are my own. But how do you know? How can you possibly know for sure? At some level, there has to be a degree of trust between us. But as more and more work, even creative work, becomes automated, we may legitimately wonder, *Who or what am I actually reading and learning from right now?* Is the cynicism in our culture only going to increase?

According to a Pew Research Center survey conducted a few years ago, public trust in the federal government has plummeted since the mid-twentieth century. In 1964, 77 percent of Americans agreed with the statement "I trust the federal government to do the right thing always or most of the time."[6] By 2017, that number had declined to 18 percent. I don't share this data to make any particular point about how much we should or shouldn't trust the government. I share this only to point out that we have a trust problem. Specifically, we have a trust-in-*authority* problem. We find ourselves here for a variety of reasons but three in particular stand out:

The expanding influence of media.
The increasing influence of technology.
The deepening influence of autonomy.

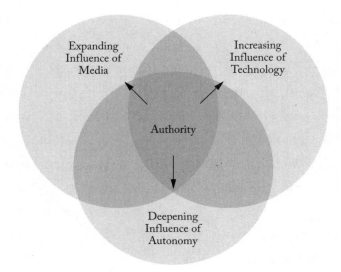

The media have been able to use technology to dissemi-
nate enormous amounts of information, and oftentimes this
information is inaccurate or untrue. Misinformation is everywhere. Meanwhile the forces of individualism cause us to push
back against any information or viewpoint that we perceive
as calling our autonomy into question. We create disinfor-
mation aimed at those who challenge us, or we isolate ourselves against views we disagree with, creating echo chambers.
Taken together, this creates an enormous amount of skepticism and suspicion, particularly of authority.

But Christians are called to speak good news expressed most
clearly to us through the authoritative words of Scripture. But
if we live in a world that questions or is even repulsed by
anything that declares itself as authoritative, what are we to do?

Sadly, the problem is compounded by some who have

misunderstood and misapplied Scripture. Some have conflated the authority of Scripture itself with interpretations of Scripture. We can, of course, debate various approaches to hermeneutics and exegesis, which helps us better understand Scripture. But ultimately Scripture isn't meant to be a sword we wield against opposing views and the people who hold them, even though that is often how Scripture is used today. That kind of use backfires. Trenches are dug in deeper, outrage increases, the screaming back and forth elevates, and we are pulled further and further apart.

So, again, what are we to do? Scripture is indeed a sword, with a particular enemy in mind. More on that in a moment. But the Bible is more than a sword. It's also a scalpel.

SURGERY BY SCRIPTURE

As I write this, dear friends are at the hospital, waiting as doctors perform cochlear implant surgery on their baby boy. I was with my friend Andy, the boy's dad, last night at the small group we belong to. We surrounded him and prayed for him, his family, and his son. Several of us prayed specifically that God would grant the surgeon immense skill and precision during surgery.

The author of Hebrews writes that "the word of God is alive and active. Sharper than any double-edged sword, it penetrates even to dividing soul and spirit, joints and marrow; it judges the thoughts and attitudes of the heart" (4:12).

In the original language of the text, *sword* is the Greek word *machaira*, and in the context of the verse, it most likely means *knife*, a common meaning of the word at the time.[7] The word of God is a knife or, put another way, a scalpel, that does surgery on us, "dividing soul and spirit, joints and marrow."

The majority of the church fathers and early medieval theologians understood that "the word" in this text refers to Jesus himself, as in the opening of John's Gospel: "In the beginning was the Word, and the Word was with God, and the Word was God" (1:1). But since the Protestant Reformation, much of the thinking has shifted, and "the word" is now often understood as the written word of God. There are valid arguments for both interpretations, but what seems clear is that "the word," whether Jesus directly or Christ expressed through Scripture, is the "agent of interior change"[8] in us human beings.

Scot McKnight writes that "God did not give the Bible so we could master him or it; God gave the Bible so we could live it, so we could be mastered by it."[9] Put another way, we read and study the Bible for the intent and purpose of inviting the God of the Bible, by his Spirit and through his Word, to diagnose what is wayward within—and to cut into us, so to speak, exposing and removing anything keeping us from living in complete surrender to Christ. This is what being mastered by the Bible looks like, a life of surrender.

And surrender always precedes *speaking*.

Before we can speak biblically in a way that will be heard in a noisy world, we must first surrender to God and allow his Word, Christ expressed through Scripture, to do necessary work within. But what does this look like?

Allow God to Do His Work

In any meaningful relationship, consistency of time and place matters a great deal. Jenny and I have a monthly date night. The kids usually stay with my mom and off we go to dinner without young children to enjoy unrushed adult conversation. It's become a necessary rhythm in our marriage, one I greatly look forward to. But without intentional planning and disciplined commitment to prioritizing the dates, the tyranny of the urgent would almost always overwhelm us.

Likewise, if we don't set aside a time to read Scripture daily, life gets in the way, and God cannot do his work in us, slowly and steadily over time.

Choosing a time and place to read the Bible, intentionally planning the rhythm of your day around this time and place, and prioritizing said time and place are all key to allowing Scripture to work in us. The time necessary is best carved out in the mad rush of daily life through quiet, committed consistency. For me, this takes place on most mornings around five a.m., in the hushed stillness of a house still waking up. I pour some coffee and read the Bible. Honestly, most mornings are unspectacular. But God often speaks quietly over time through the mundane constancy, and showing up day after day has become one of my primary modes of surrender.

Reading Together

Author and professor John Dyer, in his book *People of the Screen*, reflects on how various technological advances have affected the way people read, understand, and experience the Bible. In its earliest form, Scripture was a collection of scrolls and existed this way for millennia until they were codified into a set sequence, the codex, a few centuries after Christ. Dyer suggests that in these forms, which both existed in a predominantly preliterate world, Scripture was primarily experienced communally. People gathered to hear the reading of the Word and were invited to meditate on it together.

When Johannes Gutenberg invented the printing press in the fifteenth century, the world began its march toward literacy. In 1452, he printed 180 copies of the 1,300-page Gutenberg Bible.[10] According to Dyer, this significant technological shift moved people away from a communal experience of hearing and meditating on Scripture together toward a personal experience of reading and studying Scripture alone. This is a good thing for the most part. But as more recent technologies have digitized the Bible, Dyer suggests that we're beginning to see reading and studying begin to evolve, or devolve, into scanning and searching.

When we engage the Bible the way we engage most other digital and media platforms—scanning for bite-sized tidbits of information or inspiration, searching for immediate answers to specific problems or challenges in the moment—we find ourselves skimming the surface of Scripture at the expense of delving deeply into it. But the transformative work happens in the depths. Surgery always takes place in the places we can't easily see.

One of the best antidotes to our tendency to scan, search, and skim is to read in community. In the digital age especially, we need to recover not only the habit of personally reading and studying Scripture but also the gift of hearing Scripture together. When we explore the Bible with others, the experiences and interpretations of others can help guide us into deeper places.

Recently at our church, several dozen people gathered to read all of Paul's New Testament letters out loud together. Three hours of Scripture read, received, considered, pondered, and meditated on together as a community. It was a beautiful sound to hear and sight to behold, as the Word of God cut into us, through joints and marrow to soul and spirit, enlivening us, individually and collectively. We left that space sensing that now, just maybe, we finally had something to say.

SPEAKING TO ILLUMINATE

I think back often to the story I told at the start of this chapter about my friend Earl asking me to read him the psalms during his waning days on earth. As he peered into the oncoming darkness of death, he knew that Scripture could light the path before him until he arrived safely on the bright shores of

heaven. Psalm 119, which I quoted earlier, is the most powerful reminder of the illuminating power of God's word:

> Your word is a lamp for my feet, a light on my path. I
> have taken an oath and confirmed it, that I will follow
> your righteous laws. I have suffered much; preserve my
> life, Lord, according to your word. Accept, Lord, the
> willing praise of my mouth, and teach me your laws.
> Though I constantly take my life in my hands, I will
> not forget your law. The wicked have set a snare for
> me, but I have not strayed from your precepts. Your
> statutes are my heritage forever; they are the joy of my
> heart. My heart is set on keeping your decrees to the
> very end. (vv. 105–112)

The psalms in particular are deeply emotional, though
they also offer calm in the chaos of our lives. In Psalm 119,
the author shares how he has suffered much, taking life into
his own hands and facing snares set for him by the wicked.
These are honest and humbling admissions. But each time, the
psalmist finds stability and strength in nearness to God and
his word—it is a lamp and a light, righteous, able to preserve
life, a heritage of joy. Adherence to God's word was synony-
mous with allegiance and nearness to God himself.

In the psalms we often see sudden shifts from sadness to
joy, mourning to dancing, despair to hope, but these are sudden only on the page. As Tremper Longman explains, "We

must remember that the Psalms aren't magical incantations. It sometimes appears that the psalmist changed his negative feelings to positive ones in a brief moment, but this isn't how it happened. The Psalms compress time in such a way that what was a long process appears as a sudden insight. Honest emotional struggle stands behind the Psalms."[11]

Understanding this dynamic between the psalmists' lived experience and poetic expression of that experience is crucial for speaking biblically. We often approach Scripture as if it were a flashlight, expecting to flick a switch, point, and shed immediate light on any particular situation. We expect it to work the way the words are laid out on the pages of the psalms—all of life's problems resolved neatly within a matter of a few verses. And we expect the journey from one place to the other to be as swift as reading the lines of text in our Bibles.

But the Word of God doesn't work like that. It often doesn't give an answer quickly and then we move on until we need another quick fix. The Word is a lamp—a warm, inviting, and steady illumination that works only as our eyes adjust to the light and only if we stay in close proximity. It shows the best way forward at the pace of a steady walk, not a run. Speaking biblically in order to illuminate requires a willingness to move at this sort of pace.

Followers of Jesus must embody the spirit of Scripture, patiently and gently speaking into people's lives with grace, truth, compassion, and conviction. It means entering into the pain, anxiety, fear, uncertainty, suffering, and despair that others carry, often for the long haul. It would be convenient to offer a few verses with simplified theological ideas, claiming that settles everything, but this approach seldom leads to anything meaningful. It rarely illuminates.

Many of us so often rush to defend a position, conclusively react to a particular issue, or offer a terse answer to complex questions by quoting Scripture, under the false pretense that a quick word or the last word means victory or resolution. But such an approach, much like the unexpected flare of a flashlight, can blind. But lamps don't blind; they reveal. This is what speaking to illuminate looks like.

THE SWORD

In the summer of 1995, my friends and I went to see the Disney film *Pocahontas* probably a half dozen times. Well, we at least bought tickets to *Pocahontas* a half dozen times. Once in the theater, our small crew of fifteen-year-old adolescent boys would sneak in to see the R-rated movie *Braveheart*. Mel Gibson in warpaint with an epic sword. I was mesmerized. Later that year, when *Braveheart* was released on VHS, I saved up and bought it. A few years later, I purchased the DVD. It's not a stretch to guess that I've spent a hundred hours of my life watching Gibson's guttural Scottish screams as he wields his sword.

Braveheart is loosely based on the real life of thirteenth-century Scottish war hero William Wallace. At the national monument built in his honor, in Stirling, Scotland, visitors regularly file in to see the Wallace Sword, which according to legend was the sword William Wallace used to defeat the English army in 1297 at the Battle of Stirling. The sword stands nearly five and a half feet in length, leading many to believe that William Wallace was quite literally a giant. Some historians estimate that he might've been six feet seven inches in height. And this was at a time in world history when the height of an average man was just north of five feet. Wallace's sword was the size of an average man.

In his letter to the Ephesians, the apostle Paul uses battle imagery to describe the Christian life: "Be strong in the Lord and in his mighty power. Put on the full armor of God, so that you can take your stand against the devil's schemes" (Ephesians 6:10–11).

The enemy here is the devil and his "schemes," which is the Greek word *methodia*, meaning "craftiness" or "deceit." In fact when the Bible uses war metaphors and battle imagery, generally the devil is the enemy, and his craft and deceitful methods are often mentioned.

As we become more polarized, many followers of Jesus have fallen prey to the schemes of the devil. Mainly, we believe the lie of the enemy that those on the "other side" of an issue are the enemy. But Paul makes clear, "Our struggle is not against flesh and blood, but against the rulers, against the authorities, against the powers of this dark world and against the spiritual forces of evil in the heavenly realms" (Ephesians 6:12).

When we wield our sword, the sword of Scripture, against

others, we unwittingly wield the sword in allegiance to the devil. That is, when another person is the enemy, we can be certain that we are on the wrong side of the fight.

Paul continues, "Take the helmet of salvation and the *sword* of the Spirit, which is the word of God. And pray in the Spirit on all occasions with all kinds of prayers and requests. With this in mind, be alert and always keep on praying for all the Lord's people. Pray also for me, that whenever I speak, words may be given me so that I will fearlessly make known the mystery of the gospel, for which I am an ambassador in chains. Pray that I may declare it fearlessly, as I should" (Ephesians 6:17–20, emphasis added).

The sword belongs to the Spirit and is given to us as the word. It's revealing here that Paul's train of thought continues from the sword toward prayer and, specifically, the prayer that "words may be given me so that I will fearlessly make known the mystery of the gospel...that I may declare it fearlessly." Paul longs to speak the gospel and declare it fearlessly to those who are in need of good news. In essence, this passage is about using the word for the *good* of those who need the gospel.

During my first few years of college, I went through a season of deconstruction, leaving the faith of my childhood behind. Removed from the safe harbor of my youth group, meaningful Christian relationships, and the community of the local church, the loneliness and isolation of young adulthood left me dangerously vulnerable to the devil's deceptions, exploiting my hurts, traumas, and insecurities.

Growing up as the only child of an immigrant mother, I had little in the way of luxuries and comforts. We lived paycheck to paycheck, always scraping by, sometimes barely hanging on. I have immense admiration for my mother's resolve, resilience, and character. She forged a life for us out of nothing. But in the wilderness of doubt, the devil confronted me with the same sort of question he asked Jesus in the wilderness: "If God really loves you so much, why do you hunger for so much more? Why did he make it so hard on you?"

I believed the lie. A hard life must mean God doesn't really love me. And if I've been told all my life that God is love, then there must be no God. In the words of the writer Julian Barnes, my mantra became "I don't believe in God, but I miss him."[12] I'd left God because I thought he was no longer plausible, which intensified my doubt, plunging me deeper into the depths of despair, and eventually drowning me in a sort of suffering I'd not previously known. Though God was my way out, the prison of my own making was darkened by the whispers of the devil, and I could not see it.

In my weakened and desperate state, I reoriented my desires and my energy toward the pursuit of success and pleasure. I could take this prison, remake it into a little empire of my own, and achieve and enjoy my way to freedom. So I went about pursuing any and all worldly trappings I could. But it all left me wanting, and spiraling deeper into despair. I was lied to, and I was stuck.

Truth be told, at that point in my life I was an absolute

mess. I had disappointed and hurt a lot of people, and there were some people in my life who wanted nothing to do with me. I didn't blame them. Most days, I didn't want anything to do with me either.

I'd grown up in church with a handful of older guys who'd invested in me. I'd spent years of my life shooting hoops with them, sharing meals, talking about Jesus, serving, worshiping, and leading alongside them. They were men I admired and aspired to emulate. But when I deconstructed faith, I deconstructed those relationships as well. And it hurt them. I regretted the pain I caused, but I was far too ashamed to acknowledge it. I expected to live as a distant memory to them at best, and an enemy at worst.

A few years into my wilderness wandering, I was shocked when these same guys began reaching out. Eventually they invited me to join them on Monday nights, to hang out, share a meal, and reestablish relationships. And though I didn't believe what they believed, I wanted what they had—the sort of freedom, joy, and lightness of heart they seemed to exude. Over many months, through Scripture and conversation and a genuine sense of belonging, the truth of God expressed through the love and wisdom of my friends began to help disentangle me from the lies.

Rather than preach at me, they prayed with me.

Rather than make me feel dumb for not knowing what they knew, they leaned into my lack of knowledge with deep humility and shared curiosity.

Rather than tell me what they knew, they taught me to search and study Scripture.

It was truly good news for my broken soul, and it changed my life forever.

With hearts open, they extended undeserved love and grace in my direction by using the Scripture as a sword and wielding it carefully but confidently against the lies of the enemy, which had done so much destructive work in my life.

They didn't just tell me I was loved.

They showed me through the Word.

They didn't just tell me that purpose, meaning, and joy were possible and available.

They showed me through the Word.

They didn't just tell me where it had all gone wrong.

They showed me the better path forward, through the Word.

God set me free and drew me back into his family because of it.

This is the power of speaking biblically.

It is the power to cut into us and cut out of us the lies of the enemy.

It is the power to hear and be heard, to heal and be healed, to welcome and be welcomed, to transform and be transformed.

Seven

Where We Speak: Speaking in Place in a Placeless Age

In November 2022, Priscilla Sitienei passed away at the age of ninety-nine. At the time of her death, Priscilla, affectionately called Gogo, meaning "grandmother" in the local Kalenjin language, was the oldest primary school student in the world. She lived her whole life in a small village called Ndalat, in the Rift Valley of Kenya, and for almost seven decades, she served as the local midwife, helping deliver hundreds of babies. Having never had the opportunity of a formal education, in 2010, in her mid-eighties, she enrolled at Leaders Vision Preparatory School.

Six of her great-great-grandchildren were her classmates, as were several ten- to fourteen-year-olds she'd helped deliver. When asked why she wanted to go to school at her age, Sitienei replied, "I'd like to be able to read the Bible."[1] During her seven years at the school, she actively participated in English, math, PE, dance, music, and drama classes. According to classmates and the school's headmaster, she was a wonderfully engaged student, eager to learn and never hindered by the fact that she was seventy years older than the other students.

The nineteenth-century Swiss philosopher Henri-Frédéric Amiel noted that "to know how to grow old is the master work of wisdom, and one of the most difficult chapters in the great art of living."[2] Though uneducated by formal standards, Priscilla Sitienei commanded the admiration and attention of her community because she'd mastered the "master work of wisdom," growing old with grace, humility, and curiosity. The people of her village knew it wasn't an act because they knew Gogo—she'd been there, after all, for nearly a hundred years. When she passed, there was immense grief and celebration for a life well lived in the one and only place she ever called home.

The place I've called home almost my entire life, the Bay Area of California, experienced its initial population boom in the mid-nineteenth century, when gold was discovered in San Francisco. Between 1846 and 1850, the population of the city grew from less than one thousand residents to more than twenty-five thousand hopeful transients looking to get in, get rich, and get out.[3] In the past half century, Silicon Valley has become the epicenter of digital technology, and as a result the world has converged on my backyard. The *get in, get rich, get out* ethos of the original gold rush continues to thrive.

Due to a variety of factors, including but not limited to cost of living, the near impossibility of home ownership, and lack of space, many people have moved away or are planning on leaving. In the first two years of the COVID-19 pandemic, between March 2020 and the early spring of 2022, ninety thousand residents moved away,[4] bringing the population down to a ten-year low.

Many people have good reasons to move. It's hard to live here. I get it. This chapter isn't a manifesto on staying. Sometimes leaving is the right thing to do. "Pick up and go to the land I will show you," God might say. And sometimes, staying is the easy, convenient, lazy, or even ungodly thing to do, even if you're paralyzed by risk aversion. Sometimes staying is like burying the treasure God gave you to steward in the sand. To be where God calls you, whether that means staying or going, is and always will be the right place.

But in our day, as options abound, the grass over there always seems so much greener than the grass right here, and we find ourselves perpetually unsettled, beckoned over and over again by the possibilities of what life could be like in that other place. Even when we're not looking for that new life, our attention wanders to other places. Laptop open. Work being done. And in a moment of boredom or stress, we open up a new tab to Southwest or Airbnb. Maybe even Zillow. We find reprieve from the tedium of *right here* via the intoxicating escape of *over there*. But the consequence of our desire to escape is ultimately rootlessness.

In our world of transience, though, one of the most powerful ways to be heard is to be rooted, committed to a particular place and a particular people. Place matters, probably more than we realize especially in our hyperdigitized, disconnected, always on but rarely present world. Speaking good news in a way that can be heard today requires more than a captive audience; it demands relationships, rooted in a place we care for. But this sort of rootedness is challenging today, in large part because we're losing our aptitude for healthy attachment.

DETACHED

The US surgeon general Vivek Murthy notes that "loneliness and weak social connections are associated with a reduction in lifespan similar to that caused by smoking 15 cigarettes a day."[5] According to some researchers, a single cigarette decreases life expectancy by eleven minutes.[6] The math tells us then that a single day feeling lonely or without a sense of deep social connection robs us of about two and a half hours of life. One year in this state takes more than forty days of life. A decade lived in loneliness is actually less than nine years of life.

And yet, many continue on in their search for greener pastures at the expense of a life rooted in deep relationships. The fourth-century Stoic philosopher Seneca once famously said, "Everywhere means nowhere. When a person spends all his time in foreign travel, he ends by having many acquaintances, but no friends."[7] Though Seneca said this with regard to reading, arguing that we need to read broadly, the general principle applies to us in our placeless age.

Everywhere is actually *nowhere*. One of the most deceptive illusions of the digital age is the belief that we can be everywhere, all the time, all at once. Until the internet, the concept of place was always and only applied to a specific physical location. But in our digital world, physical limits can be transcended by a few clicks, scrolls, or swipes. We find ourselves tempted to escape physical spaces for virtual ones. And because we believe we can be everywhere, many live with a pervasive sense of placelessness, a feeling that we are actually nowhere at all.

More important, as the concept of place has shifted, our sense of belonging and communal responsibility has shifted along with it. Our always on, always ready digital devices beckon us to leave our physical place in the real world and go everywhere. We are in fixed locations, but as our attention ventures off into a digital world, we find ourselves living in perpetual detachment from real community.

On a very basic level the internet promises connection, a nearness to others that is able to bridge physical, geographic, cultural, and even linguistic divides. And so we all go online, longing for meaningful relationships as well as safety and security. Indeed, this is what we all want.

What is fascinating is that a quarter century ago, many feared that with all of us going online, the internet would lead younger generations toward more inappropriate behavior— more drugs, sex, and rock and roll. The technology would enable them to indulge debaucherous longings. But according to recent research, the opposite has happened. Younger generations are less likely than previous generations to go out without their parents, date, have sex, drink, abuse substances, or get a job.[8] This has led leading researchers like Jean Twenge to conclude that "adolescence is now an extension of childhood rather than the beginning of adulthood."[9]

Declines in teenage sex, alcohol consumption, and substance abuse are worth celebrating. But something more alarming is taking place beneath the surface. Healthy risk taking and the once adventurous spirit of young adulthood have given way to a dire and desperate search for safety in isolation, mediated almost exclusively online. The ambition or longing of Generation X and Millennials to grow up and strike out on their own have been replaced by Generation Z's and Generation Alpha's reluctance to grow up in the real world and reticence to spend extended time from the perceived security of digital confines. But these generations are not actually kept safe or secure online.

An extensive research study conducted by the CDC shows that in the ten years between 2011 and 2021, the percentage of high school students who felt persistent feelings of sadness or loneliness increased 14 percent, and suicidal ideation among teens rose 6 percent.[10] If the internet is supposed to provide for us unlimited relationships, as well as safety and security from the real world, why then are we so sad, lonely, and even suicidal? Are we not deeply separated?

In the early 2010s, when teenagers first got their hands on smartphones, the trendline of in-person time spent with friends took a nosedive. In 2010, the average American teen spent more than two hours a day with friends. By 2019, before the pandemic shutdown of 2020, that number had been cut in half.[11] Even among older generations, the percentages all drop precipitously between 2010 and today. In essence, our addiction to our devices has utterly detached us from our community.

We go to our smartphones, drawn in by the allure of nearness.

We discover a semblance of safety and security for a few fleeting moments.

But they turn out to be façades, and we eventually find ourselves separated from others and in genuine despair.

But why? Why does the promise of the internet fail?

True, meaningful relationships are anchored in consistent, loving care. We find safety and security only if and when we are seen and known.

But social and news media, personalities, pundits, and influencers seek our attention and offer us none in return. The same goes for the Zillow list of idyllic homes in ideal cities, the Airbnb excursion plans, the travel blogs, vlogs, and airline deals all enticing and tantalizing us to get away. They are one-way attachments that stimulate the senses with much to see and much to know but leave us wholly unseen and unknown.

As we attach ourselves to the hopes and dreams of a place-less life mediated on screens, devices, and the next big get-away, these very attachments leave us detached. We think we are independent and self-sufficient, but in actuality we are unable to relate and ultimately trust others. We're rootless, resulting in increasing isolation and loneliness.

Why does this matter when it comes to speaking good news in a noisy world? It matters because this isn't just me or you. It's almost everyone. When we speak, we are speak-ing to those who, like us, often feel lonely, isolated, anxious, and placeless. Being heard in a meaningful and genuine way requires relationship.

When people feel seen by us...

When people feel known by us...

When people have and hold our attention...

This is when we can finally be heard.

To truly see, know, and offer the gift of our attention requires first awareness. That is, we must be aware of the three key positions we are living in at all times with respect to the people in our life—right here, over there, and out there.

RIGHT HERE

Construction on the Tower of Pisa began in 1173. Five years into construction, as the builders were working on the third story, they noticed that the tower was leaning. They tried to compensate by shortening the uphill side of the tower. Rather than resolving the issue, it made things worse, and by the end the tower was off center by fifteen feet. Today, more than five million people visit the Leaning Tower of Pisa every year for an obligatory photo op.

What many don't know though is that in the city of Pisa, there are two other bell towers that also tilt off center, one at the Church of St. Nicola and the other at the Church of St. Michele. The reason for these leaning towers is because of Pisa's proximity to the ocean. Its subsoil is soaked in seawater. In fact, the word *pisa* actually comes from the Greek word for "marsh." These towers are built on top of a marshy foundation. But there's no way to know this by looking just at the surface. The difference between what's on the surface and the substance beneath makes all the difference, whether building a tower or speaking good news.

In 2 Corinthians 13:5, the apostle Paul writes, "Examine yourselves to see whether you are in the faith; test yourselves." In the original Greek, the sentence actually begins, "Yourselves, examine." Paul does this for emphasis. Self-examination is the starting point for any Christian, and without it much of what we speak out into the world will offer little to no substantive help to others.

David Brooks writes that developing a consistent point of view that can bring about good in the world begins "with an awareness of the constant presence of egotism, self-centeredness, and self-deception."[12] Speaking in a way that can be heard begins by paying careful attention to what's happening right here, in us.

Before we speak to the world, we listen to God speaking to us and enter the dialogue. We invite him to expose what is hidden within us, what's hidden from others and even our own selves. Curt Thompson writes that "that which is broken was not always so; it is merely the outgrowth of defiled desire. And for the world to be redeemed, God does not destroy desire; rather, he resurrects and renews it while using it to renew everything else, beginning with us."[13] Speaking right here begins by asking God to reveal the answer to a crucial question.

"Why do I want to say what I want to say, <u>really</u>?"

_____

Right Here

"Why do I want to say what I want to say, *really*?" This question helps expose underlying desires, biases, and motivations. If we ask this question honestly and allow God to speak to us, there's no more hiding. We are exposed and we must respond accordingly.

Many know the story of King David's grotesque sin in 2 Samuel 11. "At the time when kings go off to war" (v. 1), David remained home, and one evening he sees a woman bathing from the vantage point of his palace roof. He desires her and takes her. The woman, Bathsheba, is married and now carries the child of the king, who is not her husband. David tries to cover up his sin by calling Bathsheba's husband Uriah home from war, but once he arrives, he refuses to sleep with his wife while his men are in battle. David piles evil upon evil by sending Uriah to the front lines of the war to die.

That David, who is called in the Bible a man after God's own heart (see 1 Samuel 13:14; Acts 13:22), can have such significant lapses not only in judgment but in self-awareness must be a lesson to us all. Desires, biases, and motivations can become drugs, incapacitating us and dictating our behaviors in ways we may never have intended and may not be fully aware of.

The prophet Nathan confronts the king with his grave sin. Defensiveness and justification would've been the expected response. But instead, David repents and composes one of the most enduring songs of confession in history, Psalm 51: "Have *mercy* on me, O God...my *sin* is always before me... create in me a *pure heart*, O God...restore to me the *joy* of your salvation... Then I will *teach* transgressors your ways, so that sinners will turn back to you...open my lips, Lord, and my mouth will *declare* your praise" (emphasis added).

Psalm 51 shows us beautifully yet painfully that we must first speak right here, before speaking over there and out there. In a noisy world, before we chime in and enter the fray, people of God would do well to begin by seeking the mercy of God, naming our own sin, and inviting him to remake our hearts.

What's fascinating, and perhaps entirely unexpected, is that as we experience the transformative power of God changing us, joy is the result. Then, from joy, not based on situations or circumstances but on the boundless grace of God which renews us, we can speak or teach, always in humility and gentleness, with our own sin before us, beneath the shadow of his mercy. Our speaking becomes a declaration, not simply opinions intended to win an intellectual argument or convince others of their ineptitude, but definitive proclamation of God's goodness and a plea to align ourselves to that goodness.

This is what it looks like to speak right here, to grow in self-awareness and humility. It means accepting and embracing God's honest truth about our desires, motivations, and biases and moving out into the world as grateful recipients of grace. Then and only then are we finally ready to speak to others. As Steve Cuss writes, "on the other side of self-awareness is difficult work that brings deeper freedom for us and those we serve."[14] We move now from speaking *right here* to speaking *over there*.

OVER THERE

A few years ago, a married couple asked to meet with me to discuss a leadership decision I'd made in my role at the church. They were having a difficult time coming to terms with it and wanted further clarity. There was clearly tension in the room, and I was doing my best to navigate the conversation, when all of a sudden, about half an hour in, the husband raised his voice and shouted, "I could punch you in the face right now!" Needless to say, I was taken aback. Sure, we had divergent views on the matter, but nothing in the meeting up to that point had indicated to me that such rage was burning beneath the surface. I attempted to stay calm and nonreactive on the outside, but on the inside, I felt a rush of anger and defensiveness.

In his book *Talking to Strangers*, Malcolm Gladwell writes that "with strangers, we're intolerant of emotional responses that fall outside expectations."[15] That was it. I was torn by my pastoral sensibilities, wanting to maintain peace and work toward clarity—even under threat of physical harm—but there was another side of me, a more primal, animalistic side, that couldn't stand for such antagonism.

If speaking right here is about asking God to help us grow in self-awareness, then by speaking over there we engage those who are close to us or with whom we come in contact on a day-to-day basis—friends, family, neighbors, coworkers, and congregants—any and all within the ripple effect of our lives.

In the words of Dallas Willard, "those around us within the range of our power to affect."[16] So how exactly are we to speak over there in a way that can be heard?

In my office that day, though this married couple and I were talking to one another, it was abundantly clear that neither of us were hearing nor being heard by the other. In his letter to the Colossians, Paul writes, "Be wise in the way you act toward outsiders; make the most of every opportunity. Let your conversation be always full of grace, *seasoned with salt*, so that you may know how to answer everyone" (Colossians 4:5–6, emphasis added). In the ancient world, a conversation "seasoned with salt" was speech that was compelling, convicting, or inviting for the listener. As one writer describes it, "Salt cannot work from a distance. To do its preserving and consecrating work, it must be rubbed into the contours, or 'hidden' into the object it works on."[17]

Physical proximity does not of course imply a close relationship. It is possible to sit inches apart from another person and be "enemies." There's often a relational gap between people. And so though I do believe that physical presence does matter,[18] it alone does not bridge the emotional or ideological differences that pull us apart. In order to season a conversation with salt, to speak effectively over there, we must somehow bridge those gaps.

But when emotions are running high and misunderstandings or disagreements abound, grace is the only antidote—refusing to become indignant when wronged, affirming the person even if their ideas may be in error. The effort needed to show grace and bridge those gaps is enormous, but one key question can help us do that work: "What am I missing that requires more attention?"

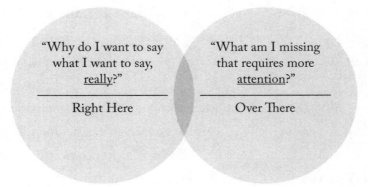

"Why do I want to say what I want to say, really?"

Right Here

"What am I missing that requires more attention?"

Over There

Speaking over there, often at the intersection between physical nearness and relational distance, requires us to focus our attention away from ourselves and toward the other. This is the critical movement that takes place from right here to over there. In his book *The Road Less Traveled*, psychiatrist M. Scott Peck notes that "The principal form that the work of love takes is attention...When we attend to someone we are caring for that person. The act of attending requires that we make the effort to set aside our existing preoccupations...and actively shift our consciousness. Attention is an act of will, of work against the inertia of our own minds."[19]

In my conversation with the couple that day, the gap between us was wide. While it would have been easier for me to blame them for misunderstanding me and misconstruing my intentions, the deeper truth is that I didn't give them my focused attention. My focus was on me, not them. And as a result, I failed to attend to them appropriately. Instead of setting aside my self-centeredness and pride, I dug deeper into them and stood emboldened in a posture of opposition. This isn't to say they were right and I was wrong. That's beside the point. But without hearing them, getting to the heart of the matter was a lost cause.

We don't control whether someone will be convinced of our point of view on any given issue. But if agreement, or at least genuine understanding, is to have a chance over there, we must move our attention off ourselves and focus it over there. This is difficult work and our failure often to make this shift has in part led to the online hellscape out there.

OUT THERE

In an article for the Gospel Coalition, my friend Patrick Miller tells the story of a woman named Sherry he met a few years back in a pastoral counseling session: "Sherry began to cry. Her husband put an arm around her, pulled her close, and said, 'It will all be okay.' It was a kind sentiment. But it was wrong. She'd lost her mother. Not to death. To Facebook."[20]

A few years prior Sherry's mother had created a Facebook profile, and the algorithms then did their work, leading

Sherry's mother into the vortex of conspiracy theories, fear-mongering, and us-versus-them propaganda. Sherry had lost her once kind and gentle mother. In his book *Truth over Tribe*, co-written with Keith Simon, Miller writes, "Keeping people angry simply requires an ever-increasing level of shrill, partisan hot takes—both from media and from the people you follow. Over time, innumerable rabbit holes open up and descend into an ever-darkening well of conspiracies, outlandish academic theories, and alternative facts that collectively begin to construct a new mental reality. This explains why your friends and family are becoming more radicalized on the internet. Big Tech is serving them more and more radical content in a bid for their attention."[21]

Speaking *right here* begins with asking God to make us self-aware and listening.

Speaking *over there* is focusing our attention on those within our spheres of effect and influence.

Speaking *out there* is about speaking effectively into the digital ether, the non-place place where we spend so much of our time.

But how on earth do we speak in a way that can be heard amid this world of hyperbolic anger, virtue signaling, and a whole lot of screaming, shouting, and name calling? Is it even possible?

One of the primary challenges of speaking out there is distinguishing between talking and doing. Speaking to be heard, in any context, involves far more than words. In the introduction of this book, I briefly drew out the difference between grabbing attention and holding attention. Holding attention, which is what speaking in a way that's actually heard does, requires active participation and commitment.

In her book *Reclaiming Conversation*, Sherry Turkle writes that while espousing partially formed opinions on any number of issues online is easy and convenient, if you want to be truly constructive and make real progress, then "you need ties of deeper trust, deeper history. You will have to move beyond gestures and donations; you will need to reach consensus, set goals, think strategically, and have philosophical direction. Lives will depend on your deliberations. Perhaps your own life. You will need a lot of long conversations."[22] This is the dilemma of speaking out there, because the internet is not designed for trust, history, and long conversations.

Turkle offers a series of what she calls "guideposts" for engaging online more effectively.[23] The last of these guideposts is to avoid all-or-nothing thinking. She writes, "The digital world is based on binary choice. Our thinking about it can't be...When computational possibilities are introduced, camps form and the middle ground disappears... The complexity of our circumstances calls for a flexibility of approach."[24] Speaking out there in the digital age, in a way that can be heard, cannot take place without a "flexibility of approach."

But as flexible as we may try to be when speaking online, speaking exclusively out there is ineffective and non-optimal. As Patrick Deneen writes, "What we need today are practices fostered in local settings, focused on the creation of new and viable cultures, economics grounded in virtuosity within households...Not better theory, but better practices."[25]

The best practice when speaking out there is to invite people back over here. As Turkle reminds us, "Shared solitude grounds us. It can bring us back to ourselves and others."[26] In a placeless age, when everyone is looking for escape, the best thing we can do is invite people back to a place and a community. This often means zigging when everyone online is zagging. A flexibility of approach when speaking online means:

Listening when everyone is shouting

Leaning in when everyone is piling on

Offering points of agreement as the starting point, not the finish line

Expressing curiosity instead of drawing conclusions

Seeking the pain beneath instead of adding pain to the surface

These and more are ways of asking, "Can I say this in a way that draws others in?" which is the most important question to ask when speaking out there.

PEACE AND PROSPERITY IN EXILE

Jozef de Veuster was born in 1840 in rural Belgium, the youngest of seven children. Sensing a call to ministry, he followed in the footsteps of some of his older siblings, two sisters who'd become nuns and an older brother who'd become a priest. Though de Veuster had dropped out of school at age thirteen to help on the family farm, and though some considered him too uneducated for the mission field, his natural intelligence won the day, and he eventually made his way to the Hawaiian Islands in 1864.

In Hawaii, de Veuster was ordained and took on the religious name Damien. Over the next decade he ministered faithfully and joyfully. But by the early 1870s, leprosy was ravaging his local congregation and the islands at large. Because there was no cure at the time, the Hawaiian government deported people with leprosy to the island of Molokai, where they had to live out the remainder of their lives away from family and friends, suffering terribly from pain and abandoned to a slow and lonely death.

The bishop of Hawaii at the time urged priests to courageously and sacrificially serve these people. Damien heeded the call, and in 1873, he left for Molokai, knowing well that the likelihood of a long life or any sort of return to normalcy was slim to none. He lived and served on Molokai for sixteen years. He preached the gospel; pastored and prayed for his people; built houses, schools, and roads; established hospitals and churches; and provided medical, emotional, and spiritual support. He dug graves and performed countless funerals.

Then in 1884, Damien contracted leprosy. Friends and family begged him to return home and live out the remainder of his days in some semblance of comfort, but he refused. He stayed and continued to love and serve his people until his death on April 15, 1889. Jozef de Veuster was forty-nine. In 2009, he was canonized by Pope Benedict XVI. He is most commonly known as Father Damien of Molokai.

What compels a person to go when most everyone else would stay?

What compels a person to stay when most everyone else would go?

Jeremiah was a prophet who lived six hundred years before the birth of Christ. In his day, the people of God had lost their homeland and were living in exile in Babylon. Distraught and homesick, the people assumed that God would take them home shortly. "Don't unpack the boxes. We'll be out of here in no time." But through Jeremiah, God instructs his displaced people in a surprising way.

> This is what the Lord Almighty, the God of Israel, says to all those I carried into exile from Jerusalem to Babylon: "Build houses and settle down; plant gardens and eat what they produce. Marry and have sons and daughters; find wives for your sons and give your daughters in marriage, so that they too may have sons and daughters. Increase in number there; do not decrease. Also, seek the peace and prosperity of the city to which I have carried you into exile. Pray to the Lord for it, because if it prospers, you too will prosper." (Jeremiah 29:4–7)

Build houses. Settle down. Plant gardens. Start families.

This is the language of place, not placelessness. Wherever you find yourself, even if it feels like exile, for however long God has you there, make it your home. Create gathering spaces. Plant roots. Cultivate the potential good beneath the soil and dirt. Be fruitful and multiply. Even in Babylon. Even in exile. Be a people of place.

Seek the peace and prosperity of the city to which I have called you into exile.

In a placeless age, followers of Jesus can be heard by being a people of place, rooted and committed amid the frantic, anxious rush of many to get out.

Followers of Jesus find voice by seeking the peace and prosperity of the places and the people to whom God has called us. Even on Molokai. Even in Babylon. Even in exile. Even where you are, right here, right now.

Eight

The Neighborhood Boundaries

My middle school crush was Elisabeth Shue. I should clarify, this was a celebrity crush, a pretty common thing for twelve-year-old boys. And girls. Jenny, my wife, had her fair share of celebrity crushes growing up too. She once wrote a letter to the Backstreet Boys, inviting them to perform at her birthday party. They never responded. But I digress. Back to Elisabeth Shue.

In my mid-twenties I played in an extraordinarily mediocre rock band, and one year we were down in Southern California playing at a youth conference. One afternoon during some downtime, my bandmates and I got into a discussion about *Back to the Future Part II*, which featured none other than my middle school crush as Marty McFly's girlfriend. A day later, still at the conference, the four of us got into the elevator to go up to our hotel room, and as the elevator doors opened, we noticed a lone rider. It was none other than Elisabeth Shue, standing there next to a duffel bag full of aluminum bats.

Turns out, there was a Little League baseball tournament in town, and Elisabeth Shue's kids were playing. We immediately devolved into twelve-year-old boys. We were nervous, and it felt like pimples were breaking out all over my face. We could tell that she could tell we knew exactly who she was. The ding of the elevator door disrupted our awkward silence as we arrived at her floor, and I mustered all the courage I could and said, "Can I help you with your bats?" Without making eye contact, Elisabeth Shue replied, "No thanks," and rushed out of the elevator.

This was the most memorable elevator ride of my life. But that's not saying much. Elevators aren't just boring; they're awkward, quite possibly one of the most awkward spaces human beings occupy on a regular basis. Every day, about 325 million people ride an elevator,[1] with the average passenger taking four trips.[2] This comes out to about 1.3 billion elevator rides every single day. Two out of three riders admit that they don't want to talk in an elevator.[3] Doing the math tells us that there are more than 300 billion awkward silences in elevators every year.

So why exactly are elevators like this? In the 1960s a cultural anthropologist named Edward Hall developed a field of study called proxemics, which seeks to understand how human beings relate to and interact with one another within various physical proximities. Hall posited that for any given person there are four categories of space around the body, and within each space we feel comfortable allowing only certain people with whom we share certain relationships.

Intimate space extends out from the body to about one and a half feet. Most people are comfortable with only those with whom they share an intimate relationship being this close. Spouses and children would fit in this category.

Personal space extends out to about four feet. This space is reserved for those with whom we share a meaningful personal relationship. Close friends and family are typically in this category.

Social space extends out to about twelve feet. In social settings involving both friends and strangers, we reserve the space near us for those we know well but feel most comfortable when others stand at the edges of this space.

Public space extends out to about twenty-five feet. Imagine a warm summer day at a large, open field with plenty of room. If a group of strangers chose to sit anywhere within this space when there was plenty of other space to choose from, we'd feel awkward and strange.

Elevators are awkward because they break the rules of proxemics. Our physical closeness belies our relational closeness. Strangers are not meant to share intimate physical space, but that's exactly what happens hundreds of millions of times a day. The incongruity is nearly unbearable. In the same way, the mailman would never step inside the house. Friends having lunch would never sit at different tables. Newlyweds would never get a suite with two beds for their honeymoon. We keep and close distances based on relationships. This is, in most cases, appropriate and healthy.

But speaking good news in a way that can be heard in a noisy world breaks the rules of normative expectations and takes us on an uncomfortable journey across the boundaries of the spaces we typically reserve for a select few. It begins with a jarring redefinition of who our neighbors actually are and a willingness to cross cultural, relational, and preferential borders, in order to listen and speak in love.

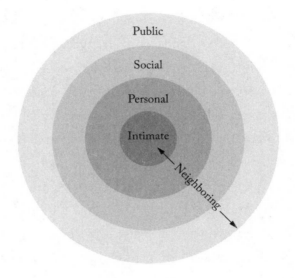

Which brings us to the Good Samaritan.

BE THE NEIGHBOR

There's a Good Samaritan Hospital a few miles from my house. It's one of more than seventy hospitals in the United States named Good Samaritan, all derived from the gospel story in which Jesus tells the parable of an unlikely neighbor, which begins like this.

On one occasion an expert in the law stood up to test Jesus. "Teacher," he asked, "what must I do to inherit eternal life?"

"What is written in the Law?" he replied. "How do you read it?"

He answered, "'Love the Lord your God with all your heart and with all your soul and with all your strength and with all your mind'; and, 'Love your neighbor as yourself.'"

"You have answered correctly," Jesus replied. "Do this and you will live."

But he wanted to justify himself, so he asked Jesus, "And who is my neighbor?" (Luke 10:25–29)

Jesus goes on to tell the famous parable of a Jewish priest and then a Levite coming upon a man robbed and battered, lying in the road, barely clinging to life. Both men, in respected positions of religious authority, pass by the man. While these first two men are often characterized as antagonists in the story, within the context of the day, they were simply doing the right thing, culturally and religiously.

The story tells us that the beaten man was "half dead" (Luke 10:30). Because of Jewish ritual laws and their religious roles in the community, the priest and the Levite were legally bound to keep distance from any form of death. Physical contact would've rendered them ceremonially unclean, which would've been an inexcusable and irresponsible act of recklessness. The man in need was legally out of bounds. It's here we meet the Good Samaritan.

> But a Samaritan, as he traveled, came where the man was; and when he saw him, he took pity on him. He went to him and bandaged his wounds, pouring on oil and wine. Then he put the man on his own donkey, brought him to an inn and took care of him. The next day he took out two denarii and gave them to the inn-keeper. "Look after him," he said, "and when I return, I will reimburse you for any extra expense you may have." (Luke 10:33–35)

Jewish and Samaritan hostilities at the time ran deep, extending back nearly a millennium. The Jews considered Samaritans half-breed heretics who'd conjured up a bastardized form of Judaism. It was commonplace for Jews to travel extreme distances on journeys simply to avoid trekking through Samaria.

By making a Samaritan the true neighbor in the story, Jesus was being provocative. As one theologian describes it, "A Jewish audience would regard it as particularly humiliating to receive such extravagant love from a Samaritan, of all people, so that Jesus's concept of neighborliness goes far beyond a patronizing benevolence."[4] This was beyond unexpected; it was ludicrous. But the most fascinating part of the story is Jesus' concluding question to the expert in the law.

"Which of these three do you think was a neighbor to the man who fell into the hands of robbers?"

The expert in the law replied, "The one who had mercy on him."

Jesus told him, "Go and do likewise." (Luke 10:36–37)

The original question from the expert had been "Who is my neighbor?" He was seeking a definitive profile. He wanted Jesus to draw the boundary lines for neighboring.

"Who is my neighbor?" is also a way of asking, "Who is not my neighbor?" Put another way, the original question is something like, "Who am I obligated to care for, attend to, and serve?" And conversely, "Who am I not obligated to?" In his brilliance, Jesus turns the question around. "Who was a neighbor to the man?"

"Who is (and isn't) my neighbor?" is the wrong question.

The right question is "Who can I be a neighbor to?"

Becoming a neighbor takes precedence over *seeking* a neighbor.

In the parable, the Samaritan breaks all the normative cultural boundaries. Samaritans and Jews weren't supposed to interact, much less come to one another's aid. This is a part of Jesus' point.

During the Rwandan genocide of 1994, Immaculée Ilibagiza, whose family was a part of the Tutsi minority ethnic group, was sent by her father to hide from the majority Hutu militia forming to hunt and kill Tutsis. She was twenty-three years old. Ilibagiza, along with seven other Tutsi women, found shelter in the home of a local pastor. For three months, they hid in a small three-by-four-foot bathroom, keeping silent and still during the daily searches by soldiers. "The bathroom became the setting for Ilibagiza's test of faith and forgiveness, which began by praying the Lord's Prayer many times a day."[5] The pastor who sheltered these Tutsi women, at risk of his own well-being, was a Hutu.

This is what it looks like when a Christian follows Jesus' seemingly impossible command. "You have heard that it was said, 'Love your neighbor and hate your enemy.' But I tell you, love your enemies and pray for those who persecute you, that you may be children of your Father in heaven" (Matthew 5:43–45). In the words of Leo Tolstoy, "Love your enemies, and you will have no enemies!"[6]

To erase the boundaries and bridge the divides of neighboring in this way is only possible with a significant shift in paradigm and perspective. As I wrote earlier, a redefinition is necessary. Paul reminds in 2 Corinthians 5:14–16 that "Christ's love compels us, because we are convinced that one died for all, and therefore all died. And he died for all, that those who live should no longer live for themselves but for him who died for them and was raised again. So from now on *we regard no one from a worldly point of view.* Though we once regarded Christ in this way, we do so no longer" (emphasis added). The phrase "worldly point of view" is two words in the Greek, *kata sarka*, meaning "according to flesh."

There are two distinct lenses through which to see people—culture and the cross. Cultures come and go, and along with them, an ever-changing, fickle, volatile set of values, arbitrarily dictating where people sit on the hierarchy of social value. But the cross is fixed in time, the fulcrum of history, and seeing people through the cross means seeing them anew. Theologian David Garland reminds us, "When we see that we are all sinners dead in our sins and needing reconciliation from God, and when we accept Christ's shameful death on the cross as our death, then all previous canons we used to appraise others must be scrapped."[7] In *The Weight of Glory*, C. S. Lewis expounds on this truth: "There are no ordinary people. You have never talked to a mere mortal. Nations, cultures, arts, civilizations—these are mortal, and their life is to ours as the life of a gnat. But it is immortals whom we joke with, work with, marry, snub and exploit—immortal horrors or everlasting splendors."[8]

Amid the polarization of our day, more of the same—more echo chambers, more partisan vitriol, more ideological hostility—only amplifies the noise drowning out the voice of God and one another. But when we redefine the boundaries of neighboring by giving ourselves to the great and painful work of loving our enemies, learning to embrace foe as friend and friend as family, we begin to attract and hold the attention of a world seeking solace from the loneliness and isolation wrought by tribalism. In a world where everyone longs to be seen as extraordinary, when ordinary people like you and me begin to identify, name, and honor the extraordinary in others, people begin to listen.

When we stop asking "Who is *my* neighbor?" and begin asking "Who can *I* neighbor?" our posture toward the world begins to change. And as our posture changes, so can the tenor of our voice, as we begin speaking with a genuine desire to draw near to those who are far from us and to bridge the divides that separate us. This can change entire communities and our own experience of belonging. As Jay Pathak and Dave Runyon note in their book *The Art of Neighboring*, "By becoming good neighbors, we become who we're supposed to be. As a result, our communities become the places that God intended them to be."[9]

SUSHI AND SNAKES

When I was in college, a close friend got a job as a waiter at a new restaurant, a renowned sushi place from Southern California that was expanding to our city. In order to make sure they got the opening right, the restaurant held a soft opening event so that the front of house, waitstaff, and kitchen crew could run a dinner service before the official public opening—essentially a dress rehearsal. My friend got a few of us in for the dinner. Anticipation was high. But the evening was disappointing. The food was just okay, not great, and the service was worse than subpar. It was chaotic, disorganized, and uncomfortable. Needless to say, we didn't have a great time. But what we didn't do was complain.

The entire staff was new. The restaurant wasn't ready to open. This was a test run. Knowing all of this, empathy was easy to come by. Most important, though, we were there to support our friend. Like all the other waiters, he was flustered and frustrated and got things mixed up. But we left him a generous tip, not because he necessarily deserved it, but because he's our friend and we were proud of him despite his struggles. We wanted him to know he was loved. We didn't have to give him the benefit of the doubt, because we already knew without a doubt that he was doing his best. We were there to cheer him on.

Among friends, the veil of anonymity is torn away. We see one another with clarity, detail, and depth. This is the difference between friendship and mere acquaintance. While acquaintances might know a bit or know of one another, friends know definitively and are known deeply by one another. Indifference, fear, and frustration are replaced by care, concern, and support. Assumptions give way to trust.

Words are only one part of the speaking and hearing experience. Relationship is the bedrock upon which the meaning of our words are planted, cultivated, and brought to life. As such, one of the greatest tactics the enemy of God can deploy against us, especially in a noisy world, is pulling the veil back over our eyes.

In Genesis 1, at the beginning of the biblical story and the beginning of the human story, God creates all things, and the pinnacle of creation is humanity. "In the image of God he created them; male and female he created them" (v. 27). This sets humans apart. No other thing in all of creation, living or nonliving, bears God's image. Human beings are not divine godlike beings. But they are also not just like everything else. They are unique image bearers. This has been true since the beginning and continues to be true today. Back to the C. S. Lewis quote from earlier: "There are no ordinary people."

In Genesis 2, we read a more detailed description of God's creative action in bringing humans to life. We discover that after God "formed a man from the dust of the ground and breathed into his nostrils the breath of life" (v. 7), he found one thing lacking in his new world. "The Lord God said, 'It is not good for the man to be alone'" (v. 18). Then the text takes a strange turn. "Now the Lord God had formed out of the ground all the wild animals" (v. 19). The Hebrew words for "wild animals" are *chayyat ha'sadeh*. Keep that in mind. God proceeds to bring all of the *chayyat ha'sadeh* to the man Adam, to be named. "But for Adam no suitable helper was found" (v. 20). Man is alone, and it's the only thing in God's good world that isn't good.

"So the Lord God caused the man to fall into a deep sleep; and while he was sleeping, he took one of the man's ribs and then closed up the place with flesh. Then the Lord God made a woman from the rib he had taken out of the man, and he brought her to the man. The man said, 'This is now bone of my bones and flesh of my flesh; she shall be called 'woman,' for she was taken out of man" (Genesis 2:21–23). The Hebrew word for "rib" is *tzela*, and in the Bible it almost always means "side," typically as an architectural reference, as in the two equal sides of the Ark of the Covenant (see Exodus 25:12), which is the next time we see the word. In fact, *tzela* wasn't first translated as the English word *rib* until long after the writing of the Hebrew Scriptures. In essence, God splits the first human and makes two distinct, complementary yet equal beings—man and woman, both bearers of his image.

Enter the serpent. "Now the serpent was more crafty than any of the wild animals the Lord God had made" (Genesis 3:1). The serpent is the craftiest of all the wild animals, all of the *chayyat ha'sadeh*. Here and in Genesis 2:19 are the only two places where this phrase shows up in the entire book of Genesis.

The serpent invites the man and woman to take and eat the fruit from the tree of the knowledge of good and evil, which God has strictly forbidden (see Genesis 2:17). This is the serpent's attempt to rob the humans of their unique role as God's image bearers, to drag the man and woman back down to the place of *chayyat ha'sadeh*, to make them just another pair of wild animals. But God had already made clear, man is not a wild animal, which is why a complementary, equal partner could not be found for him among all other earthly creatures. As Rabbi Ari Lamm puts it, "[The serpent] represents the jilted would-be soulmates of the animal kingdom. And he's here to take humanity down a peg."[10]

Still, the humans are deceived and eat the fruit that was not theirs to eat, introducing sin and death into the human story. God banishes them from the garden. But he does not send them off as just another pair of *chayyat ha'sadeh*, wild animals. "The Lord God made garments of skin for Adam and his wife and clothed them" (Genesis 3:21). God clothes sinful humans. While the serpent is cursed to "crawl on your belly and...eat dust all the days of your life" (Genesis 3:14), Adam and Eve are given the dignity of covering.

In a world pulled apart by rants and diatribes, caricaturing, minimizing, and criticizing one another, Satan continues to do his work, dragging us down into the dirt and dust of *chayyat ha'sadeh*. We see and treat one another as nothing more than wild animals, defensive and afraid, ready to kill or be killed.

Wild animals don't speak and listen. They don't hear one another. They scream, shout, snarl, growl, and roar. Theirs is a primal communication, forged by predatory, animalistic instincts designed and intended only for survival. Spend a few minutes on Twitter or watching the cable news network of your choice and you'll notice much of the same. But humans aren't wild animals. We're meant to engage and interact differently.

Richard Mouw writes:

> Every human being is a center of value. The value may not always be obvious to us. This is why we have to go out of our way to reflect on the value of specific human beings. We Christians can do this by reminding ourselves that the person in question is created by God. If an artist friend produces a work of art that I

don't particularly like, I can still treat that artifact with reverence if I remind myself of the value it has for the person who made it. The more I respect the artist, the more I will go out of my way to revere her work.[11]

Everything changes when we take the time to consider that though we may not genuinely value all equally, God does. If what Paul says is true, that "we are God's handiwork" (Ephesians 2:10), then anyone we speak to is the artwork of God. God cherishes that person. In those moments when we cannot seem to muster the necessary perspective to see this, we can speak in a way that displays respect and reverence for God himself. Doing so empowers us to step across the borders between those we love, those we tolerate, those we find challenging, and even those we and society at large have forgotten.

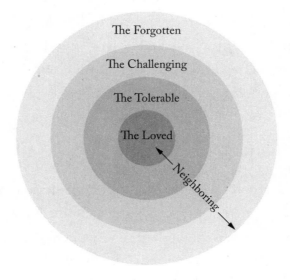

In the summer of 2012, a high-school junior runner named Meghan Vogel lost a race and yet captivated the crowd. After winning the 1,600-meter race earlier in the day, Vogel was set to compete in the more arduous 3,200-meter race for the state title. Weary and unrecovered from her previous race, she fell to the back of the pack, running in last place as she approached the home stretch. Then with about twenty meters to go, a sophomore from a competing high school, Arden McMath, collapsed on the track. Her legs completely cramped up and her body started shutting down.

This took place at the state championships. There were thousands in the stands. Vogel was already the 1,600-meter champion, and one doesn't achieve such success without a drive to win and a certain amount of ego and pride. And though she was struggling in this race, finishing last meant being the worst, and such an outcome is unacceptable to just about any high-level athlete. But Meghan Vogel did what many, maybe most, would not even think to do. She slowed down and stooped low to help a competitor up.[12]

No one would've blamed Vogel for rushing past her fallen foe, a stranger she'd never met and, for all intents and purposes, at least in the context of a race, her enemy. No one would've chided her for doing what she was supposed to do and running hard to the finish line, taking advantage of the opportune moment to save herself the humiliation of finishing last. Runners collapse and others run past in races all the time.

But Meghan Vogel crossed the boundaries of her lane,

stepped into the space of a fallen runner, picked her up, carried her across the finish line, and finished last. And in a moment, a state championship race became a vision of what can happen when community transcends competition. After the race, Vogel said, "I think fate may have put me in last place for a reason. It's strange to have people telling me that this was such a powerful act of kindness and using words like 'humanity.' I just did what I knew was right and what I was supposed to do."[13]

What if followers of Jesus could think of our place in the world this way? Not that fate but God himself has put us exactly where we are among people, circumstances, and situations we did not necessarily choose for a reason?

As the world tells us that what matters is finishing first, what if God's people could embody the beautiful truth that what matters most is finishing together?

Carrying each other when we fall is the right thing to do. It's what we're supposed to do. Even if it means crossing the lines of running lanes, even if it means crossing the boundaries of those we love, tolerate, find challenging, or have forgotten altogether.

As the boundaries are crossed, the neighborhood expands, and we find ourselves belonging to one another in the way God always intended.

The Father Speaks in Flatland

Imagine for a moment that you are a flat, two-dimensional square living in a flat, two-dimensional world. What would happen if a three-dimensional object, a sphere, let's say, were to crash into your two-dimensional reality? How would you perceive and experience this object? How would you make sense of it?

This is the premise of Edwin Abbott Abbott's 1884 book *Flatland*. Abbott wrote the book as a satirical political commentary on Victorian culture and its hierarchical limitations. Though the book was not immediately successful, it has gained influence over time for its unique storytelling and exploration of dimensions, and as an original work of mathematical fiction. But I find the narrative of *Flatland* especially helpful for articulating the struggle and tension I've experienced throughout my Christian life when it comes to hearing God's voice. It's a struggle and tension that's probably familiar to you as well.

We are finite beings marching collectively to the linear beat of time in a three-dimensional reality called human experience. But God is not.

God is infinite and not bound to the limits of time and space.

He transcends the finitude of human understanding.

He who wrote and designed the natural order of things can also rewrite that order as he pleases. This is what we mean when we say that God is supernatural.

"My thoughts are not your thoughts, neither are your ways my ways," declares the Lord. "As the heavens are higher than the earth, so are my ways higher than your ways and my thoughts than your thoughts." (Isaiah 55:8–9)

Can you find out the deep things of God? Can you find out the limit of the Almighty? It is higher than heaven—what can you do? Deeper than Sheol—what can you know? Its measure is longer than the earth, and broader than the sea. (Job 11:7–9 NRSV)

Great is our Lord and mighty in power; his understanding has no limit. (Psalm 147:5)

Oh, the depth of the riches of the wisdom and knowledge of God! How unsearchable his judgments, and his paths beyond tracing out! Who has known the mind of the Lord? Or who has been his counselor? (Romans 11:33–34)

The idea that finite humans might actually be able to hear the voice of a transcendent God is, in some ways, absurd. Attempting to comprehend his voice is akin to a flat, two-dimensional square trying to make sense of a three-dimensional sphere. How can we possibly hear the voice of God when:

His thoughts are not our thoughts.
His ways are not our ways.
His limits are unknowable.
His understanding is limitless.
His judgments are unsearchable.
His paths are beyond tracing.

What chance do we have? Is our attempt to hear God in a noisy world entirely futile? I've often found myself frustrated to the point of resignation, giving up on the hope that a vibrant, ongoing conversation with God is even possible. As Andrew Root writes, "It is easier to conceive of God only as a flat concept—a kind of final contingent relation behind the curtain of all other explanations—than to conceive of God as an acting and speaking agent in the world."[1] This has been much of my Christian life, a life of minimizing a transcendent, supernatural God and boxing him into categories that fit neatly into the confines of what makes sense in the limited natural order of things.

But God desires so much more for us. Better yet, he desires so much more with us. God is intent on establishing the vibrant, ongoing conversation we often believe isn't possible. Dallas Willard diagnoses the difference between what God wants and what we believe is possible this way: "Our failure to hear God has its deepest roots in a failure to understand, accept and grow into a conversational relationship with God, the sort of relationship suited to friends who are mature personalities in a shared enterprise, no matter how different they may be in other respects."[2]

I've come to discover that one of the primary reasons for my own struggle in hearing God is because I long for his voice only when I think I need to hear it. Rather than living in continuous communion with God, in an ongoing conversation about the big, small, and in-between stuff of life, I usually seek to hear God when I am at the end of my rope, at a loss, desperately seeking answers and solutions. God is more often than not a last resort. Willard notes that "Nothing will go right in our effort to hear God if this false motivation is its foundation. God simply will not cooperate."[3] Why? Because God is interested in relationship, not reciprocal transaction.

It's tempting to think of and approach God like a cosmic vending machine. We find ourselves in need of an answer to a particular problem or a resolution to a specific circumstance, and we go to God in prayer, push the right buttons, and, voilà, God responds with just what we need. But in such an exchange there is no deep relationship. No one stays at the vending machine. Expediency and pragmatism are its primary benefits. We get in, get what we need, and move on. The reason such an approach never works is because God isn't interested in giving us answers. God is only interested in giving us himself.

Chances are you decided to read this book because you long to hear his voice and, from there, speak in a meaningful way as a response. And I hope the book was helpful to you along those lines. But here's the more foundational truth: God wants us to be with him more than to simply hear him. He wants us to speak with him more than simply for us to speak effectively. God desires sons and daughters in relationship with him far more than he wants Christians who hear and speak well. But because we so often default to desiring the latter over the former, "even if we were to beg for a word from God, we may have so little clarity on what it should be like and so little competence in dealing with it, that when it comes it will only add to our confusion."[4]

In John 10:27–28, Jesus says, "My sheep listen to my voice; I know them, and they follow me. I give them eternal life, and they shall never perish; no one will snatch them out of my hand." The relationship between a shepherd and his sheep was at the time—and is still today—much more than transaction. Sheep have an acute ability to distinguish sounds and frequencies; they learn to recognize distinct voices quite quickly and are able to recognize and remember the tonal patterns of their shepherd, allowing them to distinguish his voice from all others. Sheep live within a social hierarchy, with their shepherd being the dominant figure in the hierarchy, not because the shepherd is domineering but because he is caring; he has their best interests in mind. Sheep from an early age learn to identify and trust their shepherd and his voice as a source of guidance and safety. Sheep rest easy knowing their shepherd is with them and for them. Listening to the voice of the shepherd is relational.

The writer Adam McHugh reminds us that "hearing is an act of the senses, but listening is an act of the will. In listening you center not only your ears but also your mind, heart and posture on someone or something other than yourself."[5] This is how we hear the voice of God, by centering our minds, hearts, and posture toward him, not for the transactional benefit of getting answers or solutions but out of relational longing, to be near God and with God, in all things at all times. "For he is our God and we are the people of his pasture, the flock under his care. Today, if only you would hear his voice" (Psalm 95:7).

Today, if only you would hear his voice.

Back in chapter 6, I briefly mentioned praying in my small group for our friend Andy, as he and his wife, Bianca, were taking their son Theo in for cochlear implant surgery. The surgery went well, and a short while later, Andy and Bianca took him back to the specialist to activate the cochlear implant. Theo would be hearing his parents' voices for the very first time. After months of prayer, countless consultations, exhaustive discussions, and painstaking deliberations, the day had finally arrived.

In a small room at Stanford Hospital, these two young parents sat with a boy they loved more than spoken words could ever express, and waited to see if, after ten months of quiet, he'd finally hear the voices that had been speaking their love to him since before he'd entered the noise of our world. The audiologist activated the cochlear implant, and then they said to their son:

"Hey, Theo. Hey, buddy."

"Theo. Can you hear mama?"[6]

After a moment of surprise, Theo immediately looked at his mom, his face smiling as wide as east is to west. Then a few moments later, he looked at his dad, grinning ear to ear. Though he was hearing these voices for the first time, they were voices he knew. These were the voices of love that spoke to him, saturating his heart and mind since before he'd breathed his first breath. His face expressed the beautiful paradox of confused joy and unknown familiarity. Though his ears had never heard these voices, his heart had known them since the beginning. Finally, with childlike wonder, Theo began speaking in response; the innocent, incoherent, and marvelous sounds of a ten-month-old expressing love.

Amid the cacophony and chaos, my prayer for us all is that we might attune ourselves to the voice of God, who loves us and has loved us since before we came into this noisy world; that we'd listen for the voice of love and recognize it as the voice that has been speaking all along, since before time began, drawing us close, guiding us along, and going before us; and that we'd speak with confidence, courage, and conviction, knowing that we never speak alone. God is with us, for us, speaking to us—in order to speak through us.

May we listen, listen some more, and speak.

Acknowledgments

Jenny, Harper, and Simon, our little family is God's greatest gift in my life. This book, like anything else helpful I've ever made, was a team effort, made possible in large part because of your love, kindness, and generosity. May we continue listening well and speaking good news together.

Mom, thank you for teaching me that God's voice can be heard just as clearly in the long plateaus of ordinary life and the quietness of the valleys as it can on the mountaintops of joy.

WestGate Church, this book is the result of the many conversations, sermons, and discussions we've had in recent years. Your voice is as much a part of this as mine. I'm grateful to be a part of a listening community like ours.

WestGate staff and elders, serving alongside you is one of the great joys of my life. Thank you for your infectious joy, humble spirit, and deep hunger for God and what he's up to in our lives, our church, our city, and our world. Onward.

To the many friends, old and new, who've shaped my life and ministry over the years, I wish I had the space to include each and every one of your names individually. But the fact that there isn't room enough is a reminder of God's incredible gift of you, all of you, in my life over the years. Thank you.

Notes

Introduction: Cacophony and Chaos

1. Maddy Shaw Roberts, "Scientists Created the Quietest Place on Earth, a Concrete Chamber Where You Can Hear Your Blood Move," Classic FM, April 8, 2021, https://www.classicfm.com/discover-music/worlds-quietest-room-microsoft-anechoic-chamber.

2. Aran Ali, "How Media Consumption Has Changed over the Last Decade (2011–2021)," Visual Capitalist, April 28, 2021, https://www.visualcapitalist.com/how-media-consumption-has-changed-in-2021.

3. Bo Burnham, *Bo Burnham: Inside*, Netflix, 2021.

4. H. D. M. Spence-Jones, ed., *1 Kings: The Pulpit Commentary* (London: Funk & Wagnalls, 1909), 461.

5. Seth S. Horowitz, "The Science and Art of Listening," *New York Times*, November 9, 2012, https://www.nytimes.com/2012/11/11/opinion/sunday/why-listening-is-so-much-more-than-hearing.html.

6. Jennings Brown, "Former Facebook Exec: 'You Don't Realize It But You Are Being Programmed,'" *Gizmodo*, December 11, 2017, https://gizmodo.com/former-facebook-exec-you-don-t-realize-it-but-you-are-1821181133.

7. Jaron Lanier, *Ten Arguments for Deleting Your Social Media Accounts Right Now* (Henry Holt, 2018), 45.

8. Matt Taibbi, *Hate Inc.: Why Today's Media Makes Us Despise One Another* (OR Books, 2018), 41.

One: God's Timeless Voice amid the Rage of Personalities

1. O. Carter Sneed, "The Anthropology of Expressive Individualism," *Church Life Journal*, December 1, 2020, https://churchlifejournal.nd.edu/articles/the-anthropology-of-expressive-individualism.

2. Garrett Graff, quoted in David Bauder, "On TV, 9/11 Was Last Huge Story for 'Big 3' Network Anchors," *AP News*, September 7, 2021, https://apnews.com/article/lifestyle-arts-and-entertainment-7ad26dae42c4eaf9588b019dc51de0e3.

3. Amy Mitchell, Jeffrey Gottfried, Galen Stocking, Mason Walker, and Sophia Fedeli, "Many Americans Say Made-Up News Is a Critical Problem That Needs to Be Fixed," Pew Research Center, June 5, 2019, https://www.pewresearch.org/journalism/2019/06/05/many-americans-say-made-up-news-is-a-critical-problem-that-needs-to-be-fixed.

4. Jeffrey Gottfried, Mason Walker, and Amy Mitchell, "Americans See Skepticism of News Media as Healthy, Say Public Trust in the Institution Can Improve," Pew Research Center, August 31, 2020, https://www.pewresearch.org/journalism/2020/08/31/americans-see-skepticism-of-news-media-as-healthy-say-public-trust-in-the-institution-can-improve.

5. Tristan Harris, "The AI race is totally out of control…," Twitter, March 10, 2023, https://twitter.com/tristanharris/status/1634299911872348160.

6. John Askonas, "What Happened to Consensus Reality?" *New Atlantis* no. 68 (Spring 2022): 4–6, https://www.thenewatlantis.com/publications/what-happened-to-consensus-reality.

7. Lee Drutman, "This 1981 Book Eerily Predicted Today's Distrustful and Angry Political Mood," *Vox*, January 6, 2016, https://www.vox.com/polyarchy/2016/1/6/10725086/promise-of-disharmony.

8. David Brooks, "America Is Having a Moral Convulsion," *The Atlantic*, October 5, 2020, https://www.theatlantic.com/ideas/archive/2020/10/collapsing-levels-trust-are-devastating-america/616581.

9. Quoted in Taibbi, *Hate Inc.*, 126.

10. Tremper Longman III, *Genesis: The Story of God Bible Commentary* (Zondervan, 2016), 284–285.

11. Eugene H. Peterson, *The Message*, introduction to 1 Thessalonians.

12. Marian L. Tupy, "Human Progress: Not Inevitable, Uneven, and Indisputable," Cato Institute, October 30, 2013, https://www.cato.org/commentary/human-progress-not-inevitable-uneven-indisputable.

13. Christopher Watkin, *Biblical Critical Theory: How the Bible's Unfolding Story Makes Sense of Modern Life and Culture* (Zondervan, 2022), 551.

14. Patrick Deneen, *Why Liberalism Failed* (Yale University Press, 2018), 29.

15. John Ortberg, *Soul Keeping: Caring for the Most Important Part of You* (Zondervan, 2014), 113.

16. John Baillie, *A Diary of Private Prayer* (Scribner, 1936).

17. Timothy Keller, *Prayer: Experiencing Awe and Intimacy with God* (Penguin, 2014), 30.

18. J. B. Lightfoot, quoted in Leon Morris, *1 and 2 Thessalonians: An Introduction and Commentary*, Tyndale New Testament Commentaries 13 (InterVarsity Press, 1984), 104.

19. Keller, *Prayer*, 30.

20. Tish Harrison Warren, *Liturgy of the Ordinary: Sacred Practices in Everyday Life* (InterVarsity Press, 2016), 21.

21. Warren, *Liturgy of the Ordinary*, 23.

22. C. S. Lewis, *The Last Battle* (New York: HarperCollins, 1956), 183.

Two: God's Daily Voice amid the Predictions of Pundits

1. Andrew Mercer, Claudia Deane, and Kyley McGeeney, "Why 2016 Election Polls Missed Their Mark," Pew Research Center, November 9, 2016, https://www.pewresearch.org/fact-tank/2016/11/09/why-2016-election-polls-missed-their-mark.

2. "Pollster Eats Bug after Trump Win," CNN, November 12, 2106, https://www.youtube.com/watch?v=O9Xksz3i2mg.

3. Caroline Beaton, "Humans Are Bad at Predicting Futures That Don't Benefit Them," *The Atlantic*, November 2, 2017, https://www.theatlantic.com/science/archive/2017/11/humans-are-bad-at-predicting-futures-that-dont-benefit-them/544709.

4. Beaton, "Humans Are Bad at Predicting Futures."

5. J. Richard Eiser and Christine Eiser, "Prediction of Environmental Change: Wish-Fulfillment Revisited," *European Journal of Social Psychology* 5, no. 3 (1975): 315–322, https://onlinelibrary.wiley.com/doi/abs/10.1002/ejsp.2420050305.

6. N. R. Kleinfield, "A Glimpse of the Year 2000," *New York Times*, January 10, 1982, https://www.nytimes.com/1982/01/10/us/a-glimpse-of-the-year-2000.html.

7. Steve Cuss, *Managing Leadership Anxiety: Yours and Theirs* (Thomas Nelson, 2019), 63–64.

8. Alexander Gamme, "Basic Needs—Extreme Happiness," YouTube, March 29, 2012, https://www.youtube.com/watch?v=vC8gJ0_9o4M.

9. A. W. Tozer, *Knowledge of the Holy*, 88.

10. Wendell Berry, *What Are People For? Essays*, Kindle ed. (Counterpoint, 2010), loc. 74.

11. Warren, *Liturgy of the Ordinary*, 23.
12. Karen Swallow Prior, *On Reading Well: Finding the Good Life through Great Books* (Brazos Press, 2018), 16.

Three: The God Who Sees in the "See-Me" World of Influencers

1. Leigh Stein, "The Empty Religions of Instagram," *New York Times*, March 5, 2021, https://www.nytimes.com/2021/03/05/opinion/influencers-glennon -doyle-instagram.html.
2. Taylor Lorenz, "Where Everyone's an Influencer," *The Atlantic*, July 31, 2019, https://www.theatlantic.com/technology/archive/2019/07/where-everyones -an-influencer/595213.
3. Taylor Lorenz, "Rising Instagram Stars Are Posting Fake Sponsored Content," *The Atlantic*, December 18, 2018, https://www.theatlantic.com /technology/archive/2018/12/influencers-are-faking-brand-deals/578401.
4. Lorenz, "Rising Instagram Stars Are Posting Fake Sponsored Content."
5. Lorenz, "Rising Instagram Stars Are Posting Fake Sponsored Content."
6. Lorenz, "Rising Instagram Stars Are Posting Fake Sponsored Content."
7. Jonathan Haidt and Jean M. Twenge, "This Is Our Chance to Pull Teenagers Out of the Smartphone Trap," *New York Times*, July 31, 2021, https:// www.nytimes.com/2021/07/31/opinion/smartphone-iphone-social-media -isolation.html.
8. Henri Nouwen, *In the Name of Jesus: Reflections on Christian Leadership* (Darton, Longman, and Todd, 1989).
9. "Slavery in Ancient Rome," British Museum, n.d., https://www.britishmuseum .org/exhibitions/nero-man-behind-myth/slavery-ancient-rome.

Four: Screaming to Belong

1. Jonathan Haidt, "Why the Past 10 Years of American Life Have Been Uniquely Stupid," *The Atlantic*, April 11, 2022, https://www.theatlantic .com/magazine/archive/2022/05/social-media-democracy-trust-babel /629369.
2. M. J. Crockett, "Moral Outrage in the Digital Age," *Nature Human Behaviour* 1 (November 2017): 769–771, https://www.nature.com/articles /s41562–017–0213–3.epdf.
3. Ashley Charles, *Outraged: Why Everyone Is Shouting and No One Is Talking* (Bloomsbury Circus, 2020), 81
4. Crockett, "Moral Outrage in the Digital Age."

5. Sean Illing, "A Decade of Revolt," *Vox*, December 26, 2019, https://www.vox.com/policy-and-politics/2019/12/26/21004797/2010s-review-a-decade-of-revolt-martin-gurri.

6. Parker Palmer, *A Hidden Wholeness: The Journey toward an Undivided Life* (John Wiley & Sons, 2004), 58–59.

7. Stephen Hawkins, Daniel Yudkin, Miriam Juan-Torres, and Tim Dixon, "Hidden Tribes: A Study of America's Polarized Landscape," More in Common, 2018, https://hiddentribes.us/media/qfpekz4g/hidden_tribes_report.pdf.

8. Richard Weissbourd, Milena Batanova, Virginia Lovison, and Eric Torres, "Loneliness in America: How the Pandemic Has Deepened Epidemic of Loneliness, and What We Can Do About It," Making Caring Common Project, downloadable from https://mcc.gse.harvard.edu/reports/loneliness-in-america.

9. Weissbourd et al., "Loneliness in America."

10. Weissbourd et al., "Loneliness in America."

11. "The Loneliness Epidemic Persists: A Post-Pandemic Look at the State of Loneliness among U.S. Adults," Cigna Group, n.d., https://newsroom.cigna.com/loneliness-epidemic-persists-post-pandemic-look.

12. Jonathan Haidt and Jean M. Twenge, "This Is Our Chance to Pull Teenagers Out of the Smartphone Trap," *New York Times*, July 31, 2021, https://www.nytimes.com/2021/07/31/opinion/smartphone-iphone-social-media-isolation.html.

13. Daniel Ruby, "71+ Instagram Statistics for Marketers In 2023 (Data & Trends)," Demand Sage, March 6, 2023, https://www.demandsage.com/instagram-statistics.

14. Jonathan Haidt, "The Dangerous Experiment on Teen Girls" *The Atlantic*, November 21, 2021, https://www.theatlantic.com/ideas/archive/2021/11/facebooks-dangerous-experiment-teen-girls/620767

15. Sherry Turkle, *Alone Together: Why We Expect More from Technology and Less from Each Other*, (Basic Books, 2011).

16. Rosaria Butterfield, *The Gospel Comes with a House Key: Practicing Radically Ordinary Hospitality in Our Post-Christian World* (Crossway, 2018), 62.

17. Malcolm Gladwell, *Talking to Strangers: What We Should Know about the People We Don't Know* (Little, Brown, 2019), 50.

18. Dietrich Bonhoeffer, *The Cost of Discipleship* (Macmillan, 1951), 185.

19. Curt Thompson, *The Soul of Shame: Retelling the Stories We Believe about Ourselves* (InterVarsity Press, 2015), 29.

20. For a fascinating look at Jesus' humor hidden within the Gospel texts, check out Elton Trueblood's *Humor of Christ* (Harper and Row, 1964).
21. Daryl Van Tongeren, *Humble: Free Yourself from the Traps of a Narcissistic World* (The Experiment, 2022), 148–149.
22. Eugene Peterson, *A Long Obedience in the Same Direction: Discipleship in an Instant Society* (InterVarsity Press, 1980), chap. 4.
23. Bonhoeffer, *The Cost of Discipleship*, 185.
24. Arthur C. Brooks, "Live Like the Ancient Cynics," *The Atlantic*, January 20, 2022, https://www.theatlantic.com/family/archive/2022/01/cynicism-modern-ancient-true-meaning/621314/.
25. Peter Steinke, *Uproar: Calm Leadership in Anxious Times* (Rowman & Littlefield, 2019), 8.

Five: Why We Speak: Speaking Good News

1. Neil Postman, *Amusing Ourselves to Death: Public Discourse in the Age of Show Business* (Viking, 1985), 65.
2. Neal Postman, "Informing Ourselves to Death," speech to the German Informatics Society, October 11, 1990, Stuttgart, https://web.williams.edu/HistSci/curriculum/101/informing.html.
3. N. T. Wright, *Simply Good News: Why the Gospel Is News and What Makes It Good* (SPCK, 2015), 2.
4. Jon Tyson, "This is the response…," Twitter, February 15, 2023, https://twitter.com/JonTyson/status/1626070485720002561.
5. Lee Grady, "What I love about this Asbury revival…," Twitter, February 14, 2023, https://twitter.com/LeeGrady/status/1625564645397303338.
6. Olivia Rheingold, "Why Students in Kentucky Have Been Praying for 250 Hours," *Free Press*, February 19, 2023, https://www.thefp.com/p/why-students-in-kentucky-have-been.
7. Gordon D. Fee, *Philippians*, IVP New Testament Commentary Series 11 (IVP Academic, 1999), 90.
8. Steve Carter, *Thing beneath the Thing: What's Hidden Inside (and What God Helps Us Do about It)* (Thomas Nelson, 2021), xxi.
9. Timothy Keller, "American Christianity Is Due for a Revival," *The Atlantic*, February 5, 2023, https://www.theatlantic.com/ideas/archive/2023/02/christianity-secularization-america-renewal-modernity/672948.
10. Bo Seo, *Good Arguments: How Debate Teaches Us to Listen and Be Heard* (HarperCollins, 2022).

11. J. R. R. Tolkien, *The Fellowship of the Ring*, reissue ed. (William Morris Paperbacks, 2012), 85.

Six: How We Speak: Speaking Biblically

1. Timothy Keller, "Nothing more important for a Christian…," Twitter, January 13, 2023, https://twitter.com/timkellernyc/status/1614024565201543168.
2. David Dark, "This is the language of spiritual abuse," Twitter, January 14, 2023, https://twitter.com/daviddark/status/1614133975680749568.
3. Maria Browning, "David Dark Is Still Questioning Everything," *Nashville Scene*, January 12, 2023, https://www.nashvillescene.com/arts_culture/books/david-dark-is-still-questioning-everything/article_1d71dc44–911b-11ed-ad8f-d7382f0e2e60.html.
4. Richard Dawkins, *The God Delusion* (Mariner Books, 2008), 51.
5. Matt Slick, "Early Church Fathers' Quotes on Scripture Alone Is Final Authority," Christian Apologetics and Research Ministry, December 14, 2011, https://carm.org/ecf-quotes-by-topic/early-church-fathers-quotes-on-scripture-alone-is-final-authority.
6. "Public Trust in Government: 1958–2022," Pew Research Center, June 6, 2022, https://www.pewresearch.org/politics/2022/06/06/public-trust-in-government-1958–2022.
7. David L. Allen, *Hebrews: An Exegetical and Theological Exposition of Holy Scripture*, New American Commentary 35 (B & H Publishing Group, 2010).
8. Allen, *Hebrews*, 286.
9. Scot McKnight, *The Blue Parakeet: Rethinking How You Read the Bible* (Zondervan, 2008).
10. "Printing Press," History.com, May 7, 2018, https://www.history.com/topics/inventions/printing-press.
11. Tremper Longman, *How to Read the Psalms* (Inter-Varsity Press, 1988), 81.
12. Julian Barnes, "Nothing to Be Frightened Of," *New York Times*, October 3, 2008, https://www.nytimes.com/2008/10/05/books/chapters/chap-nothing-to-be-frightened-of.html.

Seven: Where We Speak: Speaking in Place in a Placeless Age

1. Ed Thomas, "Kenyan Grandmother at School with Her Great-great-grandchildren," *BBC News*, January 23, 2015, https://www.bbc.com/news/world-africa-30935874.

2. Henri-Frédéric Amiel, *Amiel's Journal* (Project Gutenberg, 2005), https://www.gutenberg.org/files/8545/8545-h/8545-h.htm.

3. "Gold Rush Transforms San Francisco," National Park Service, n.d., https://www.nps.gov/places/000/gold-rush-transforms-san-francisco.htm.

4. Levi Sumagaysay, "The Silicon Valley 'Exodus' Has Erased Population Gains of the Past Decade," *MarketWatch*, February 14, 2023, https://www.marketwatch.com/story/the-silicon-valley-exodus-neared-record-dot-com-bust-levels-last-year-97724e0f.

5. Vivek Murthy, "Work and the Loneliness Epidemic," *Harvard Business Review*, September 26, 2017, https://hbr.org/2017/09/work-and-the-loneliness-epidemic.

6. Mary Shaw and Richard Mitchell, "Time for a Smoke? One Cigarette Reduces Your Life by 11 Minutes," *BMJ* 320 (2000): 53, https://www.bmj.com/content/320/7226/53.1.

7. J. W. Bertolotti, "Everywhere Means Nowhere—According to Seneca," Medium, August 11, 2022, https://medium.com/perennial/everywhere-means-nowhere-according-to-seneca-f0afbaf2f412.

8. Data taken from Jean Twenge, *iGen: Why Today's Super-Connected Kids Are Growing Up Less Rebellious, More Tolerant, Less Happy—and Completely Unprepared for Adulthood* (Atria, 2017), 17–47.

9. Twenge, *iGen*, 41.

10. "Youth Behavior Risk Survey: Data Summary and Trends Report, 2011–2021," Centers for Disease Control and Prevention, https://www.cdc.gov/healthyyouth/data/yrbs/pdf/YRBS_Data-Summary-Trends_Report2023_508.pdf.

11. Viji Diane Kannan and Peter J. Veazie, "US Trends in Social Isolation, Social Engagement, and Companionship—Nationally and by Age, Sex, Race/Ethnicity, Family Income, and Work Hours, 2003–2020," *SSM—Population Health* 21 (March 2023), https://www.sciencedirect.com/science/article/pii/S235282732200310X.

12. David Brooks, *The Road to Character* (Random House, 2015), 237.

13. Curt Thompson, *The Soul of Desire: Discovering the Neuroscience of Longing, Beauty, and Community* (InterVarsity Press, 2021), 24.

14. Steve Cuss, *Managing Leadership Anxiety: Yours and Theirs* (Thomas Nelson, 2019), xiv.

15. Malcolm Gladwell, *Talking to Strangers: What We Should Know about the People We Don't Know* (Little, Brown, 2019), 182.

16. Dallas Willard, *The Divine Conspiracy: Rediscovering Our Hidden Life in God* (HarperCollins, 2009), 205.

17. Joseph Rhea, "The Ministry of Salt," Mere Orthodoxy, March 24, 2023, https://mereorthodoxy.com/the-ministry-of-salt.

18. See Jay Y. Kim, *Analog Church: Why We Need Real People, Places, and Things in the Digital Age* (InterVarsity Press, 2020), and Jay Y. Kim, *Analog Christian: Cultivating Contentment, Resilience, and Wisdom in the Digital Age* (InterVarsity Press, 2022).

19. M. Scott Peck, *The Road Less Traveled: Anniversary Edition* (Touchstone, 2012), 120–121.

20. Patrick Miller, "'I Lost My Mom to Facebook': How to Shepherd a Flock Being Formed by Algorithms," Gospel Coalition, August 24, 2022, https://www.thegospelcoalition.org/article/lost-mom-facebook-shepherd-algorithms.

21. Patrick Miller and Keith Simon, *Truth over Tribe: Pledging Allegiance to the Lamb, Not the Donkey or the Elephant* (David C. Cook, 2022), 88–89.

22. Sherry Turkle, *Reclaiming Conversation: The Power of Talk in a Digital Age* (Penguin, 2015), 298.

23. Turkle, *Reclaiming Conversation*, 319–330.

24. Turkle, *Reclaiming Conversation*, 329.

25. Patrick Deneen, *Why Liberalism Failed* (Yale University Press, 2018), 197.

26. Turkle, *Reclaiming Conversation*, 326.

Eight: The Neighborhood Boundaries

1. "National Talk in an Elevator Day," TKE, n.d., https://www.tkelevator.com/us-en/company/insights/national-talk-in-an-elevator-day.html.

2. "Fact Sheet," National Elevator Industry, n.d., https://nationalelevatorindustry.org/wp-content/uploads/2019/02/Fact-Sheet.pdf.

3. Ebony Bowden, "Elevator Chitchat Off Limits, with Most of Us Riding in Silence: Study," *New York Post*, August 1, 2019, https://nypost.com/2019/08/01/elevator-chit-chat-off-limits-with-most-of-us-riding-in-silence-study.

4. R. T. France, *Luke*, Teach the Text Commentary Series (Baker Books, 2013), 191.

5. Katelyn Beaty, "I Met the Man Who Killed My Entire Family," *Christianity Today*, August 31, 2017, https://www.christianitytoday.com/ct/2017/august-web-only/i-met-man-who-killed-my-entire-family-rwandan-genocide.html.

6. Leo Tolstoy, *Delphi Complete Works of Leo Tolstoy (Illustrated)*, Kindle ed. (Delphi Classics, 2013), loc. 114935.

7. David E. Garland, *2 Corinthians*, New American Commentary 29 (Broadman & Holman, 1999), 284.

8. C. S. Lewis, *The Weight of Glory* (HarperOne, 2001), 46.

9. Jay Pathak and Dave Runyon, *The Art of Neighboring*, (Baker Books, 2012), 25–26.

10. For a fuller explanation of the profound thing happening in this part of the Genesis story, check out Ari Lamm's wonderful February 3, 2023, Twitter thread explaining the story here: https://twitter.com/AriLamm /status/1621507990842134529.

11. Richard J. Mouw, *Uncommon Decency: Christian Civility in an Uncivil World* (InterVarsity Press, 1992), 26.

12. Doug Binder, "Prep Runner Carries Foe to Finish Line," ESPN, June 4, 2012, https://www.espn.com/high-school/track-and-xc/story/_/id/8010251 /high-school-runner-carries-fallen-opponent-finish-line.

13. Binder, "Prep Runner Carries Foe to Finish Line."

Conclusion: The Father Speaks in Flatland

1. Andrew Root, *Churches and the Crisis of Decline: A Hopeful, Practical Ecclesiology for a Secular Age* (Baker Academic, 2022), 11.

2. Willard, *Hearing God: Developing a Conversational Relationship with God* (InterVarsity Press, 2015), 35.

3. Willard, *Hearing God*, 33.

4. Willard, *Hearing God*, 30.

5. Adam McHugh, *The Listening Life: Embracing Attentiveness in a World of Distraction* (InterVarsity Press, 2015), 19.

6. Bianca Nichole Wright, "Cochlear Implant Activation Day," TikTok, March 21, 2023, https://www.tiktok.com/@biancanicholewright/video /7213195839395745067.

About the Author

Jay Y. Kim serves as lead pastor at WestGate Church in the Silicon Valley. He is the author of *Analog Church*, winner of the Gospel Coalition's First-Time Author Award, and the follow-up *Analog Christian*, winner of *Outreach Magazine*'s Leadership Resource of the Year award. Jay also serves on the leadership team of the ReGeneration Project and hosts the *Digital Examen* podcast and Barna's *Making Space* podcast. He lives in the Silicon Valley with his wife, Jenny, and their two children.